SPACEMAN

SPACEMAN

THE TRUE STORY
OF A YOUNG BOY'S JOURNEY
TO BECOMING AN ASTRONAUT

Adapted for Young Readers

MIKE MASSIMINO

DELACORTE PRESS

Visit us on the Web! rhcbooks.com

Educators and librarians, for a variety of teaching tools,
visit us at RHTeachersLibrarians.com.

Library of Congress Cataloging-in-Publication Data
Names: Massimino, Mike, author.
Title: Spaceman : the true story of a young boy's journey to becoming an astronaut / Mike Massimino.
Description: First edition. | New York : Delacorte Press, [2020] | Audience: Ages: 9 to 12.
Identifiers: LCCN 2019015873 (print) | LCCN 2019020552 (ebook) |
ISBN 978-0-593-12088-0 (ebook) | ISBN 978-0-593-12086-6 (trade hardcover) |
ISBN 978-0-593-12087-3 (library binding)
Subjects: LCSH: Massimino, Mike—Juvenile literature. | Astronauts—
United States—Biography—Juvenile literature. | United States. National Aeronautics and Space Administration—Juvenile literature. | Hubble Space Telescope (Spacecraft)—
Juvenile literature.
Classification: LCC TL789.85.M324 (ebook) | LCC TL789.85.M324 A3 2020 (print)
DDC 629.450092 [B]—dc23

The text of this book is set in 12.25-point Apollo.
Interior design by Trish Parcell

To my mother and father:
You were outstanding students but neither of you had
the opportunity to go to college. However, you made
it possible for me to get an education and always
encouraged me to pursue my dreams.

I flew to space on your wings
and am forever grateful to you both.

With love, Mike

CONTENTS

INTRODUCTION

Since the publication of *Spaceman: An Astronaut's Unlikely Journey to Unlock the Secrets of the Universe,* I have visited many schools, libraries, and bookstores. A question I often get from younger people is: "But what kept you going after NASA rejected you three times?" I respond with a story from my days in graduate school at MIT. I was making dinner in my apartment before a night of studying. I had the television news on in the background, and they were showing an interview with some astronauts. I took a break from cooking to watch. When I saw the astronauts floating in the space shuttle answering questions, I thought, "That is exactly what I want to do." No question. I had clarity. Being an astronaut was the job for me.

Almost immediately, another thought entered my mind: "But you will never get a chance to do that, becoming an astronaut is impossible." That is the way I felt about it a lot of the time, that I was pursuing something that could never happen. But that was not true. It was not impossible. It was just unlikely or really hard. If I were to look at it mathematically, the chances of my becoming an astronaut were maybe one out of a million, or 0.000001, which is a non-zero number and by definition possible. The only way that 1 at the end of that string of zeros becomes a zero and then by definition my chances of becoming an astronaut would become 0.0, or impossible, was if I gave up. Once you give up, you know the outcome—it won't happen. It is impossible. I encourage young people to think about that 1 at the end of the string of zeros and not give up on their dreams.

I started thinking about rewriting *Spaceman* for young readers because I wanted to emphasize more of the formative experiences from my younger years that led me to the astronaut program. I have received many nice letters from readers. Here is a bit of one that stood out and touched me:

> Your book has inspired me to never give up on my dreams. I am about to move to another state and I'm a little nervous but your book taught me that sometimes things are scary but if you try you can get through it.

I was six years old when I watched Neil Armstrong take those first steps on the moon in July of 1969. The exploits of Armstrong and his fellow astronauts totally captivated me. I wanted to grow up and become an astronaut. But I had no idea how that could happen, so my dream faded after about a year. As I grew up, however, my interest in math, science, and space exploration persisted and blossomed, and eventually I earned an engineering degree in college. Pursuing my passions led me back to my six-year-old dream of becoming an astronaut, and my studies put me in a position where becoming an astronaut was a possibility. I have learned that education can make possible what at first might seem impossible. It is possible for someone to fulfill a dream they have as a kid or to discover and pursue a dream career that never crossed their mind until they learn about it later in life. I now have a new dream. I hope that after reading this book, *you* will be inspired to never give up. If I can realize my little-kid dream, you can realize yours, too.

A SCIENCE-FICTION MONSTER

On March 1, 2002, I left Earth for the first time. I got on board the space shuttle *Columbia* and I blasted 350 miles into orbit. It was a big day, a day I'd been dreaming about since I was seven years old, a day I'd been training for nonstop since NASA had accepted me into the astronaut program six years earlier. But even with all that waiting and planning, I still wasn't ready. Nothing you do on this planet can ever truly prepare you for what it means to leave it.

Our flight, STS-109, was a servicing mission for the Hubble Space Telescope. We were a crew of seven, five veterans and two rookies, me and my buddy Duane Carey, an Air Force pilot. We called him Digger. Every astronaut gets an astronaut nickname. Because of my last name everybody called me Mass.

Ours was going to be a night launch. At three in the

morning, we walked out of crew quarters at the Kennedy Space Center to where the astro van was waiting to take us out to the launchpad.

We got on, everything pitch-black all around us. The only light on the horizon was the shuttle itself, which got bigger and bigger as we approached, the space shuttle with its two solid rocket boosters and its massive rust-orange fuel tank, all lit up from below with very bright floodlights.

The driver pulled up to the launchpad, dropped us off, and then turned and hightailed it out of the blast zone. The seven of us stood there, craning our necks, looking up at our gigantic spaceship towering seventeen stories high above the launchpad. I'd been out to the space shuttle many times before for training, running drills. But all those previous times, there was never any gas in the tank, the liquid oxygen and liquid hydrogen that is the rocket fuel. The fuel tank is not filled until a few hours before the launch, because once you add rocket fuel it turns into a bomb sitting on the launchpad, and the area is cleared except for a few technicians who will help strap the crew into the shuttle. Usually a hub of activity, it now seemed almost deserted.

The shuttle was making these unearthly sounds. I could hear the fuel pumps working, steam hissing, metal groaning and twisting under the extreme cold of the fuel, which is hundreds of degrees below zero. Rocket fuel burns off at very low temperatures, sending huge billows of water vapor that look like smoke pouring out. Standing there, looking up, I could feel the power of this machine that had now come alive. It looked like a beast waiting there for us.

The full realization of what we were about to do was starting to dawn on me. The veterans who'd flown before, they were in front of me, high-fiving each other, getting excited. I stared at them like *Are they crazy? Don't they see we're about to strap ourselves to a bomb that's going to blow us hundreds of miles into the sky?*

I need to talk to Digger, I thought. Digger's a rookie like me, but he flew F-16 fighter jets in the Gulf War. He's not afraid of anything. He'll make me feel better. I turned to him, and he was staring up at our rocket ship with his jaw hanging down, his eyes wide-open. It was like he was in a trance. I said, "Digger."

No response. "Digger!"

No response. "Digger!"

He shook himself out of it. Then he turned to me. He was as white as a ghost. He looked the way I felt.

I am often asked if I was ever scared going into space. At that moment, yes, I was scared. Up to that point, I'd been too excited and too busy training to let myself get scared, but out there at the launchpad it hit me.

From the bottom of the launch tower, we took an elevator up to the access level, the 195-foot level. I made one last pit stop at a steel toilet bathroom up there—the Last Toilet on Earth, we call it—and then I waited. One at a time, the ground crew takes each astronaut across the space shuttle access arm, the gangway between the launch tower and the shuttle itself, and straps them into the space shuttle. Our commander, Scott Altman went first, followed by Digger and three more of my crewmates. Then it was my turn, and I was escorted across the access arm to the small white room where I was helped with putting on my parachute harness. Then I waved goodbye to my family on the closed-circuit camera and went through the shuttle hatch and into the shuttle. The hatch leads to the mid-deck; up a small ladder is the flight deck. Neither deck is very big; it's pretty cozy inside the shuttle. Four astronauts, including the pilot and commander, sit on the flight deck for launch. They get windows. The remaining three of us were on the mid-deck.

Once I was inside, the ground crew strapped me in. They helped me affix my helmet to my orange space suit. I checked my oxygen and my gear. Then I just lay there on my back for a few hours while the spaceship was readied and checked. On the mid-deck, there aren't any windows, so there's nothing to look at but a wall of lockers. I played a couple of games of tic-tac-toe on my kneeboard with my crewmates next to me, along with a few rounds of rock-paper-scissors. Then the countdown was down to thirty minutes. Then ten minutes. Then one minute. Then it got serious. The beast that terrified me out on the launchpad? Now that beast was waking up. At six seconds, you feel the rumble of the main engines lighting. The whole stack lurches forward for a moment. Then at zero, it tilts back upright again and that's when the solid rocket boosters light and that's when you go. It's *bang!* and you're on your way. You're going 100 miles an hour before you clear the tower, and accelerate from 0 to 17,500 miles an hour in eight and a half minutes.

I could not believe that people could build something so powerful.

It takes eight and a half minutes to make it into orbit. Eight and a half minutes is a long time to sit and listen to the deafening roar of the engines, feeling the shuttle shake and shudder as it fights to break out of the Earth's atmosphere. You get up to a max of three g's for about two and a half minutes at the end and you feel like you weigh three times your body weight. It's as if you have a pile of bricks on your chest or three big dudes sitting on you at the playground. The whole thing can be summed up as controlled violence, the greatest display of power and speed ever created by humans.

After we left the Earth's atmosphere, and the main engines cut off, the fuel tank released from the shuttle. We heard these two muffled explosions through the walls of the shuttle—*fump! fump!*—and then the fuel tank was gone and the whole launch experience was over as abruptly as it began. The roar stops, the shuddering stops, and it's dead quiet, except for the cooling fans from some of the equipment gently whirring in the background. Everything around you is eerily, perfectly still. You're in space.

The first thing I did was ask myself, *Am I still alive?* It took me a moment to answer. *Yes, I'm still alive.* We'd made it, safely. It took me a minute or two to get my bearings. I was still strapped in, but I could feel myself become light and float up off my seat a little into the straps. I looked to my right and saw the pen I had played tic-tac-toe with floating next to me on the end of its lanyard.

Then, once I felt acclimated, I reached up and took my helmet off and—just like I'd watched Tom Hanks do in *Apollo 13*—I held it out and let it go, and it floated in front of my face, weightless.

PART 1

I WANT TO GROW UP
TO BE SPIDER-MAN

1

A PERFECT GOOD

During my first week as an astronaut, my astronaut class-mates and I got lucky. An astronaut reunion was being held at the Lyndon B. Johnson Space Center. All the living legends from the Mercury and Gemini and Apollo programs would be there, including Neil Armstrong, the first man to walk on the moon. My hero. Everyone's hero.

Our training manager put in a request asking if Neil would come and speak to our class. He said he would but that he would speak only to us, the new astronauts; he didn't want some big public event with tons of people showing up.

Except I wasn't an astronaut yet, technically. When you first join NASA, you're an astronaut candidate, an ASCAN. For Neil's talk, the ASCANs gathered in the astronaut conference room, Room 6600 in Building 4 South. It's a very special room. Every NASA flight gets its own patch, commemorating the mission with the names of the astronauts who flew it. On the walls of that conference room, there's a plaque of every patch of every mission going back to Alan Shepard's first Mercury flight in 1961. You can feel the history of the space program when you walk in. The goal of every astronaut who comes through is to get your name on that wall before you leave. We clustered around the conference table like eager schoolkids, and Neil came in and spoke. He was older but not ancient, thinning hair, glasses, suit and tie. He seemed warm and approachable, but at the same time, he was someone you'd approach only with the utmost respect. When he got up to speak, he was very soft-spoken, almost shy.

He talked to us for about fifteen minutes, and the whole time he didn't say anything about walking on the moon, not one word about being an astronaut—nothing. Instead, he talked about his days as a test pilot at Edwards Air Force Base in California, flying the X-15, the hypersonic rocket plane that set speed and altitude records in the 1960s by flying fifty miles above the Earth, the outer limit of the atmosphere, the edge of space. That was how Neil Armstrong seemed to think of himself: as a pilot. Not as the first man to walk on the moon but as a guy who loved to fly cool planes and was grateful for the opportunity to have done it.

By focusing on his test pilot days and not on the moon landing, I think he was trying to tell us that life is not about achieving one great goal, because once that is over, life keeps going. What motivates you then? The important thing is having a passion, something you love doing, and the greatest joy in the world is that you get to wake up every day and do it. For him it was flying. He said, "Yeah, I got to fly to the moon, but I also got to fly the X-15." Just the fact that he got to go out and fly those planes every day, that's what had made him the happiest.

After he spoke, he took a few questions and said he'd sign pictures for us. He stood at the front of the conference table, and we lined up to shake his hand and get his autograph. I was toward the back of the line, and I noticed as I got to the front that every single person, when they got to the end of the table, did the exact same thing: They told him where they were when they watched him walk on the moon. I was thirty-three when I became an ASCAN, one of the youngest in the class, which meant everyone in line was old enough to remember the moon landing, and everybody had a story to tell him. Because everyone on Earth knows where Neil Armstrong was on July 20, 1969, so why not tell him where you were that day?

I decided I was going to do something different. When my turn came, I shook his hand and I said, "So is this what happens every time you meet people? They tell you where they were when you walked on the moon?"

"Yeah."

"You get it a lot?"

"Yeah, all the time."

"Does it ever bother you?"

He shrugged. "Nah, it's okay."

I never told Neil Armstrong where I was when he walked on the moon. But I remember where I was exactly, because it was the moment that changed my life. I was six years old, about to turn seven, sitting around the black-and-white TV in our living room with my parents and my sister, Franny, who was thirteen. She was wrapped up in her pink robe and I was in these baseball pajamas with pinstripes, worn and faded hand-me-downs I'd gotten from my cousins. My grandparents lived upstairs, and they came down to watch the moon landing with us.

I was glued to the television. Watching Neil Armstrong take those first lunar steps completely grabbed my mind and soul. But seeing it on TV almost made it seem normal, like it could have been any old TV show. Going outside afterward made me think about how incredible it was. I remember standing in my front yard and staring up at the moon for the longest time, thinking, *Wow, there are people up there, walking around.* To a six-year-old kid in the suburbs on Long Island, it was the most awe-inspiring experience in the world.

Neil Armstrong and Buzz Aldrin and Michael Collins,

they were space explorers. People were going to read about them hundreds of years from now the same way we read about Albert Einstein today. Those men became my heroes. They were the epitome of cool.

From that moment on, I became obsessed with space. It was all I thought about. It was all I talked about. At my school's summer recreation program, we had a space parade in honor of the moon landing. The kids were dressed up in space-related costumes. I wanted to go as an astronaut. My mother was a seamstress. She took a gray elephant costume she'd made for me for my first-grade play, cut off the tail, and added some of my dad's Army medals and an American flag on the left arm. We traded in the cardboard elephant ears for a plastic Steve Canyon jet helmet, added safety goggles, and we had my astronaut costume.

My brother, Joe, was working in downtown Manhattan that summer, and one day on his break he went to FAO Schwarz toy store and got me an Astronaut Snoopy toy. It was about eight inches high, decked out in a full Apollo space suit, including helmet, life support system, and moon boots. I still remember watching Joe walking home from the bus stop with the Snoopy box in his hands. I opened it up right there in the driveway. That whole summer, I played spaceman in the backyard, running around in the costume my mom had made, with my Astronaut Snoopy as my copilot. I played with that little guy until his enamel was cracked and worn and one of his legs broke off. (I still have him, only now he's been to space for real.)

I was obsessed with learning more about astronauts. The public library was right around the corner on Lincoln Road, and I'd go over in the afternoons and read anything I could find about the space program. They didn't have much, but whatever they had I probably checked out and read four or five times. They had a book about the original Mercury Seven astronauts called *We Seven,* and another about Gus Grissom, who'd died in the fire that killed the crew of *Apollo 1* on the launchpad at the Kennedy Space Center. I read *Time* magazine, *Life* magazine, whatever they had, whatever I could get my hands on.

That fall I started second grade, and all I talked about at school was space. I'd become a total space expert. My best friend back then—and still to this day—was Mike Quarequio, whom we called Q. He remembers me showing up for second grade and walking into class talking about spacewalking suits, the cooling systems they used, how the life support worked. I was known as "the boy in class who knows the most about space." I knew who the astronauts were, which kinds of rockets were used on which flights. I knew everything about space that a seven-year-old kid on Long Island could possibly know.

Even though I was obsessed with space, I never got into Flash Gordon or Buck Rogers or any of that. Space colonies and multiple dimensions and flying around with rocket packs—it was too far-fetched. What I loved was the science fiction of Jules Verne novels, like *Journey to the Center of the Earth, 20,000 Leagues Under the Sea,* and *From the Earth to the Moon.* Jules Verne's stories felt real. It was science fiction, but I felt it was plausible, as if it was set in the real world. In *Journey to the Center of the Earth,* they're digging their way down with pickaxes and shovels. In *From the Earth to the Moon,* a lot of what Verne predicted about space travel was accurate, from the type of metal they used to build the spaceship to the way they launched with the rotation of the planet to gain extra speed. And he was imagining all of it back in 1865!

I wasn't interested in the fantasy of space travel. I was interested in the reality of space travel. I was interested in how people got to space here and now, and at that point the only way to get to space was to join NASA, get an American flag on your left shoulder, and strap yourself into a Saturn V rocket. I had only one problem: Where I came from, kids didn't grow up to be astronauts.

My grandparents were Italian immigrants. My father's father, Joseph Massimino, was from Linguaglossa, near Mount Etna in Sicily, and he came over in 1902 to New York City and ended up buying a farm upstate in a town called Warwick, which is where my father, Mario Massimino, grew up. When my dad left the farm, he moved to the Bronx, where he met my mom, Vincenza Gianferrara. Her family was from Palermo, also in Sicily, and they lived in Carroll Gardens, an Italian neighborhood in Brooklyn. She and my dad got married in 1951. He was twenty-eight, she was twenty-five.

Although my dad never went to college, while he was working, he started taking fire safety courses at New York University and eventually became an inspector for the New York City Fire Department. His job was fire prevention. He would go into apartment buildings and businesses and make sure they had the right number of extinguishers and sprinkler systems and safety exits. He was a smart guy who did a good job and kept moving up, to eventually become the chief of fire prevention for the entire New York City Fire Department. My mom stayed home to take care of the kids, for which she deserves a medal.

My parents lived in the Bronx, which is where my older brother and sister were born, but soon after that, my parents decided to leave the city. They bought a house at 32 Commonwealth Street in Franklin Square, Long Island, which is where I came along. I was born on August 19, 1962. My brother was ten years older than me and three years older than our sister. I was a "surprise" baby. My mother used to tell me that I must have come for a reason because she thought she was done having kids after my brother and sister.

Franklin Square is right outside Queens on Hempstead Turnpike. When I was growing up, the neighborhood was filled with Italian Americans—the Quarequios, the Milanas, the Adamos, the Brunos. Ours was a big, extended Italian family. My mom had only one sister, Connie, who stayed in Brooklyn, but my dad had five sisters, who all settled somewhere in Queens or Long Island. My uncle Frank and aunt Ange lived right across the street from us, and my uncle Tony and aunt Marie were around the corner. My uncle Romeo and aunt Ann were nearby in College Point, Queens. I had aunts and uncles and cousins around all the time.

Franklin Square was blue-collar. Lots of guys worked for the city. Some kids went away to college, but most of them enrolled at the local school while living at home. My cousin Peter is crazy smart, and when he got into Princeton, my aunt Sally burst into tears and cried and wailed and begged him not to go because she didn't want him leaving the family to go to school in New Jersey.

My world was very small. People didn't think about leaving Long Island, let alone going to space. My buddy Q's dad was a pharmacist and his mom was a schoolteacher; he was one of the few friends I had whose parents had been to college. My parents always encouraged me to do whatever I wanted, but—being a fire inspector and a seamstress—there wasn't much they could do to help me become an astronaut.

I wanted to go to the Hayden Planetarium at the American Museum of Natural History more than anything; it was a big day when my mom and dad took me there. I brought home pictures of the planets and books on astronomy. But that was my only exposure to the world of space. How you got to join NASA or what college you should go to in order to get there—I didn't know anyone who could answer those questions. There was no science club at school where we could build and launch rockets. None of my friends were into space; it was something I did on my own. I had my spaceman costume, my Astronaut Snoopy, and my library books, and that was it. I didn't even know anyone who had a telescope.

Even if I had, I wasn't the most obvious candidate to become a person who gets launched into orbit. Part of the reason I idolized astronauts was because they were everything I wasn't. They were fearless adventurers, and I was an awkward kid. By the time I hit junior high, my vision was bad. I wore glasses. I was so tall and so skinny I could have been my own science experiment: If you wanted to know where the bones are on the human body, all I had to do was take off my shirt and I could show you.

Astronauts coming back from space had to splash down in the water, and I hated the water. I didn't know how to swim that well. Because there was no fat on my body, whenever my parents took us to the beach or to the local pool, it was like getting into an ice bath. I was scared of heights, too. Still am. Standing on a balcony four or five stories up and looking over? No, thank you. I didn't like roller coasters, either. They're scary. Hanging upside down? It makes you sick. Who wants to do that? I wasn't any kind of thrill seeker at all.

I had this fantasy about going to the moon, but that's all it was: a fantasy. The whole idea of actually joining NASA and going to space was so far-fetched and so far removed from my life that it was hard for me to stay interested in it. None of my friends seemed interested, and I wanted to be hanging out with my friends. What they cared about was baseball, and I loved baseball. My best friends and I played every year while growing up in the Franklin Square Police Boys Club Baseball League starting at age seven.

Soon I was as deep into baseball as I'd ever been into space. I was always throwing a ball. If I didn't have anyone to play with, I'd throw it against the stoop for hours, pretending I was pitching in a big game. The moon was 238,900 miles from Earth, but Shea Stadium was only twenty minutes away down the Long Island Expressway. My dad and I went to a lot of games, usually with my uncle Romeo and my cousin Paul.

As I got older, the whole astronaut fantasy went away. It burned bright and burned out, like many childhood dreams do. It was the same for the rest of the country. The Apollo program stopped in 1972. By then, the thrill of the space race was over. America had won and people moved on. I did, too. The astronomy books went back to the library, my Astronaut Snoopy went on a shelf, and by fifth grade I'd mostly forgotten about space. For a kid like me, being who I was, coming from where I came from, saying "I want to grow up to be an astronaut" was like saying "I want to grow up to be Spider-Man."

How the heck do you do that?

2

MOST ALL-AROUND

In my senior year of high school I applied to the engineering school at Columbia University on the Upper West Side of Manhattan. That November I went there for an interview, and the minute I arrived, I felt like I understood what college was all about. Before that, to me, college was something that people did to get a good job; but walking on that campus on this beautiful fall day, seeing the students hustling around and going to class, I had a revelation: This is where people learn. This is where you become someone. I'd never had that feeling before.

To be honest, I didn't know if I belonged at an Ivy League school like Columbia. Growing up, I was never the smartest kid in class. I was a good student, but I wasn't exactly a genius. I liked science and math. I played sports, but I was just okay. My greatest talent was for people. I wasn't one of the popular kids, but I got along with almost everybody. I was enough of an athlete to hang with the jocks and the cheerleaders. I played the trumpet in band, which got me in with the band kids. I was in advanced math, so I could eat lunch with the smart kids. I moved in a lot of circles, had pockets of friends in every group, and learned how to mix and work with different people.

I've always been curious about other people's lives. I find them interesting. I meet people and I want to know their story, what makes them tick. And the fact that I could hang out with different kinds of people helped make me a well-rounded person. I wasn't the smartest or the most athletic. I was the most all-around. If anything, it was my talent for getting along that made me stand out in school. At a parent-teacher conference, Mr. Stern, my eleventh-grade social studies teacher, said to my mom and dad, "Mike should think about applying to an Ivy League school. I think he'd do well." My parents came home and told me what he'd said, and that was the first time it had ever occurred to me to think of going to Columbia.

I submitted my application, but I didn't think I'd get in. I'd applied to a couple of schools on Long Island and I was convinced that's where I'd end up. Then one day a few months later, I was at home, sitting on the toilet, when my mom came and knocked on the door. "You got a letter from Columbia." She slid it under the door and I opened it up. When I read the word "Congratulations," I started screaming. I was going to Columbia as a freshman that fall.

Columbia opened up a new world for me. I was only a few miles from home, but it was as if I'd landed on Mars. There were students from other countries, from fancy prep schools. Even Barack Obama was on campus at the same time I was. (I never got to meet him, unfortunately, as I imagine being best pals with the future president of the United States would have some advantages.) As exciting as this new world was, I didn't fully embrace it right away. Whatever potential Mr. Stern saw in me, I hadn't found it in myself. I didn't take advantage of everything I was being offered. The summer after my freshman year, when the other kids took internships or went to study abroad, all I wanted to do was go back home. I moved back in with my parents and got a job as a laborer in Rath Park, which is the park in Franklin Square where we used to play ball. I picked up trash, mowed the grass, cleaned toilets.

Change doesn't come easy for me. I liked my hometown. I was comfortable there. It was hard for me to leave, and I think deep down I knew that doing well at Columbia would mean leaving. Being an A student at an Ivy League school would put me on a new path. I was afraid it was going to pull me away from my hometown and my friends whether I wanted it to or not.

For my major, I'd picked industrial engineering. I liked the fact that it had a mix of hard science and traditional engineering courses along with courses in economics and business. Industrial engineering also included something I found interesting: human factors, which focuses on designing machines and systems with human operators in mind.

I did fine my freshman and sophomore years, but junior year the coursework got harder and I hit a wall. It was bad. I got clobbered in Circuits and Systems, an electrical engineering course. The midterm counted for a quarter of the final grade. The average for the class was somewhere in the 80s. I got an 11. On another midterm I got a 15.

Failing those tests turned out to be a good thing. It was a wake-up call. Struggling in school was nothing new for me. For example, in eighth grade I was taking Earth Science. It was the first formal science course for me, and it was a big step up academically. I was doing so poorly that even getting extra help from my teacher, Mrs. Katz, didn't seem to make a difference. She had a suggestion. The high school National Honor Society had a tutoring program where students would tutor junior high school students. She suggested I work with a high school student. So one Saturday a tutor came to my house and showed me a new approach to understanding Earth Science. He also explained how I could improve my study habits. With his help, Mrs. Katz's help, and a renewed motivation to study as hard as I could, I was able to improve my grade. That lesson paid off for me throughout school. I learned that school is hard, and if you are struggling, it is not because you are stupid. It is because learning is not easy. Reach out and get help when you need it.

Soon after becoming as astronaut, I was invited back to my elementary school, John Street School, for a career day. It was wonderful. The students decorated the school in a space theme and were excited to welcome me back. My fourth-grade teacher, Mrs. Oko, was still teaching at John Street and came to the auditorium to have lunch with me. She said that she was having breakfast with her young son that morning and mentioned to him that she was going to see one of her former students who was now an astronaut. He commented that I must have been really smart. Mrs. Oko said she told him that although she assumed I must have been bright, if I was really smart she would have remembered. She added that she told him that being the smartest isn't always the most important trait in school or in life; working hard, having a positive attitude, and getting help when you need it can be more important for being successful. "Mrs. Oko," I said, "I couldn't agree more."

I was forced to decide what I wanted that third year at Columbia. At first I honestly thought about giving up. I contemplated changing my major from engineering to something less technical; I didn't think I could hack it. But then I started thinking about my father, working as hard as he did for the city to give me the chance to go to college. We couldn't afford for my dad to take the Long Island Rail Road in to work. It was too expensive. He was on his way before dawn every day to take the bus and the subway to the city. I didn't want him to have done it all these years just for me to give up. I also didn't want to end up doing that myself.

So I went back to class and buckled down, studying as hard as I could. I went to a completely different level. The course teaching assistants were great. They spent extra time with me, going over everything. My friends let me share their notes and spent hours helping me out. On the second midterm for Circuits and Systems, I got an 80. On the third, I got a 100. I went from the lowest score in the class to the highest. That semester, I turned everything around. I made the Dean's List for the first time.

I also started thinking about the space program again. We were entering the shuttle era. NASA had started doing drop-test flights out at Edwards Air Force Base in 1977 and had been flying operational space missions for over a year. The shuttle itself was very cool. It wasn't some tin can being launched into orbit. It was a real, honest-to-goodness spaceship. It took off like a rocket with up to seven astronauts, orbited the Earth, and gave the astronauts a place to live and work for one to two weeks. It was used to launch huge pieces of equipment and satellites, conduct experiments, and bring the results back to Earth. It was a sign that the space program was taking its next giant leap.

To me, the most exciting development was the new astronaut corps, which was full of interesting people: thirty-five in the first class, as opposed to seven for Mercury. And astronauts weren't just military test pilots anymore. The candidate pool had grown far wider. It included women and people of color. There were new faces at NASA, a new story to tell. Sally Ride had been chosen to be the first American woman in space, and her flight was scheduled to happen that summer. The anticipation surrounding her flight was huge. She was on every magazine cover and every news show. We were entering a new space age, and America was excited again.

Even with these new people joining the astronaut corps, I still wasn't thinking I'd ever be an astronaut; that dream was dead and gone. But some of my professors at Columbia started talking about how aerospace companies like Lockheed, Grumman, McDonnell Douglas, and Martin Marietta were getting big government contracts to work on the space shuttle systems. I thought maybe I could work as an engineer for NASA or one of those companies supporting the astronauts as a part of the bigger team.

Near the end of my junior year, I submitted applications to every engineering company on Long Island, and I got a summer job at Sperry, located in Lake Success, not far from Franklin Square. Sperry made everything from military hardware to office typewriters to electric razors. It was perfect. I could live at home, save some money, and still get some actual, hands-on experience.

At Sperry I met another important person in my life: Jim McDonald, an engineer who worked a few desks over. I walked up to his desk to ask a work question and ended up hanging out there for over an hour; I don't think we even got to the work question. Jim had a big crop of straight hair parted to the side and a friendly, whimsical smile. We hit it off immediately, and he became something of a mentor. More than a mentor, really—a guardian angel. He started watching over me, checking in on me when I was back at school, always making sure I was on the right path.

Sperry was my first experience with being an adult. My official job title that summer was "engineering aide," what you'd call a paid internship now. My team designed inventory systems and conveyor belts for military warehouses. It wasn't exactly exciting. I had to dress like a grown-up and drive to work. Every morning, I, along with hundreds of engineers, would file into this big building, work at a desk, go home, and come back the next day and do the same thing. Over and over and over again. Lunch was the high point of the day.

Some people want that. They like the routine, the safety of a paycheck every two weeks. But it wasn't for me. It didn't give me the sense of purpose I was looking for. As I got to know Jim McDonald better, I realized he didn't care for it, either. Jim was not a typical engineer. He was very philosophical, more interested in the person he was talking to than the work that needed talking about. One day he said to me, "You're not enjoying this, are you?"

"No, not really," I said.

"Look, Mike. You don't want to end up here. I've been here ten years. I've got a mortgage, a kid. It's too late for me. I love my family. I do things on the side to keep life interesting, but you've still got a chance. You need to find something that you're passionate about. Follow your bliss."

He pointed to a guy a few desks away who was sitting there, bored, reading some science-fiction novel. "You see that guy?" Jim said. "That guy just got his master's from Cornell. Do you know how smart he is? And look at what he's doing. You don't want that to happen to you."

For some reason, like Mr. Stern, Jim McDonald saw something in me, some kind of potential. I hadn't thought seriously about being an astronaut since I was seven years old. At that point the dream was dead. Jim opened the door for it to come back to life. That whole summer, right up to the last day I left and headed back to Columbia, he kept pushing me. "Go and do something different," he'd say. "Go to grad school. Find something meaningful. Find something important. Whatever you do, don't come back here."

3

WHO YOU GONNA GET?

When my final semester at Columbia came around, my boy-hood astronaut dream was still dormant. Then, one Satur-day evening in January 1984, my whole world changed. I was home in Franklin Square for the weekend, and my girlfriend Carola and I decided to go to the movies to see *The Right Stuff.* From the balcony of a theater in Floral Park we watched the story of the original Mercury Seven astro-nauts: Alan Shepard, the first American in space. John Glenn, the first American to orbit the Earth. These fearless test pilots pushing the envelope, risking their lives to help America win the space race against the Soviets.

It was *awesome.* The astronauts weren't just doing this big, important service for their country, they were also having a blast. They were flying fighter jets through the clouds, racing convertibles across the California desert, wearing leather jackets, smiling behind their cool aviator sunglasses. They were risking their lives every single day on the job. They were the baddest guys I'd ever seen. I didn't take my eyes off the screen for one second.

One scene in particular had a deep impact on me. John Glenn is all set to be the first American to orbit the Earth, but his launch is aborted. Vice President Lyndon Johnson is waiting outside Glenn's house, demanding to bring in TV crews to talk to Glenn's wife, Annie, on national television. But Annie has a stuttering problem; she doesn't want to be on TV. So John gets on the phone with her and basically tells her it's okay if she wants to tell the vice president of the United States to get lost. Some suit from NASA jumps down Glenn's throat, telling him he can't blow off the vice president like that. Glenn won't back down. So the NASA guy threatens to yank him out of the flight rotation and replace him if he won't toe the line. Then the other Mercury guys step up and get in the suit's face, and Deke Slayton says, "Oh, yeah? Who you gonna get?"

Finally, Alan Shepard tells the suit, "Step aside, pal." They've got Glenn's back.

That moment, to me, summed it up. That's how you treat your buddies. You stand up for each other. You stand up for what's right. I saw that and I said, "I want to be one of those guys." I wanted to go to space, but more than that, I wanted to be part of that team, to have that camaraderie, that shared sense of purpose that comes from doing something big and important. That's what was really cool about that movie—that and the view from space. When John Glenn is in his capsule looking down on Earth, the expression of wonder on his face, that floored me. The second I walked out of the theater, I knew: I wanted the whole enchilada. I wanted to be an astronaut.

My next thought was: *How the heck am I going to make that happen?* I was on the verge of graduating from college, but because my astronaut dream had been dormant for so long, I hadn't mapped out my education with space travel in mind. Columbia is a great school and it gave me a great education and a solid foundation, but back then, it wasn't a traditional pipeline to the astronaut program. I was also an industrial engineering major, which didn't seem like the right major for becoming an astronaut at all; I felt that I should have done mechanical engineering or aerospace engineering.

I had made one good decision. Back when I was working at Sperry, Jim McDonald had told me about the Program in Science, Technology, and Society at MIT. I sent off my application and I waited. I didn't do it with any thought of being an astronaut; at that point I hadn't seen *The Right Stuff* yet, and being an astronaut was still the last thing on my mind. But if you do want to be a part of the space program, MIT is one of the best schools to attend. By total coincidence, I'd taken at least one step down the right road.

While I waited to hear about grad school, I started looking for work. I still wanted to follow my father's example and work in public service. One week, IBM came to campus to recruit students from the engineering school, and I talked to one of the interviewers about their public sector office, which worked with nonprofit institutions to set up and service their computer systems. I felt like that might be interesting and rewarding at the same time.

IBM asked me to come in for an interview, but the day before I was scheduled to go, I got a letter from MIT. When I opened it (I wasn't on the toilet this time), I was shocked: They actually let me in.

The next morning, I went for the interview with IBM and it went well; the job was mine if I wanted it. I told the interviewer about the MIT offer, and he said IBM employees took leave to go to school all the time. I could defer school, work for IBM for a couple of years, then take a leave to go to MIT, and they would save my job for me. I just had to figure out what worked better: MIT now and work later, or work now and MIT later.

The first thing to do was to visit MIT. I called my dad, who took a day off from work, and we drove up to Cambridge to meet with the director of the Program in Science, Technology, and Society. He was a weird-looking academic type with crazy hair. We started talking and he seemed confused as to how I had ended up in his office.

Apparently, I hadn't read closely enough when I was researching the program. It wasn't a part of the engineering school. It was a political science degree. We were in the political science department. My father looked at me and said, "What are you doing in the political science department?"

I'd applied to the wrong grad school.

I didn't even know MIT *had* a political science department. Science, Technology, and Society, it turned out, was a program for people who wanted to write papers on how science is affecting society. The similar-sounding but totally different program in the engineering school was called Technology and Policy. It was also about how technology impacts society, but it was for engineers and scientists who actually want to design and build things. MIT allowed me to resubmit my application to the engineering school, and luckily, I got in there, too.

Even with that sorted out, I wasn't sure what to do. I'd applied to MIT only because Jim McDonald had told me it might be a good idea. I never expected to actually get in. I had no idea what I would study there, what my research would be. I hadn't thought about any of that. I didn't have any way to pay for it, either. I didn't have any scholarship or fellowship, and I knew my parents couldn't foot the bill. IBM had a great training program, and working there would keep me in New York near home. Plus, I knew I could take the job and earn money to go to grad school later. MIT felt like this huge unknown, a stretch, a risk. IBM felt like the safe choice.

I made the safe choice.

After graduation, I moved back in with my parents and commuted every morning on the train to IBM's building at Fifty-Seventh and Madison in Manhattan. The job seemed to suit my personality well. I was the technical side of the sales team assigned to the Port Authority account. Once or twice a week I'd go down to the World Trade Center, work with their information technology team, take people to lunch. The sales team was also responsible for the entertainment at IBM's monthly branch meetings. We'd put on little skits about the slow elevators and the bad food in the cafeteria. I was making a decent salary and people were treating me like a grown-up. And IBM was a great company: They took care of their people. But something was missing. I didn't have that sense of purpose I was looking for.

Then, *The Right Stuff* came out on HBO. My parents didn't have HBO, but my friend Mike Q did. He let me make a VHS tape of the movie. Every night, I'd come home on the train, pop the tape in the VCR, and watch it—and I mean literally *every* night. I'm not exaggerating. I'd watch Chuck Yeager push his Lockheed NF-104A up and up and up to the edge of space only to come crashing back down to Earth—and still walk out alive, chewing a stick of Beemans gum. Then the next morning, I'd wake up, get on the train, and go back and sit at my desk.

Going to IBM wasn't a mistake. It was something I needed to do in order to realize it wasn't what I wanted to do. Carola and I were getting serious, and I figured we were going to get married. If I stayed where I was, we'd end up living in New York somewhere, taking the train every day, and that would be it. I was only twenty-two years old, still living at home with my parents, and I could already see my whole life being over, mapped out and done.

One year after graduating college, during the last week of July in 1985, I decided to drop in and see Jim McDonald, my old mentor from Sperry, on the way to a Mets game. We went out and played catch in the street for a few minutes. We were tossing the ball back and forth, and he asked, "What's going on with you?" I told him about IBM, making the sales calls at Port Authority, doing skits for the branch meetings. He stood there and gave me this look.

"What's the matter with you?" he said. "Imagine the conversations we'd be having right now if you'd decided to go to graduate school. You'd be telling me about hearing lectures from Nobel Prize winners. You'd be telling me about the exciting new research you're working on. MIT is the opportunity of a lifetime. Instead, you're telling me about what, doing skits in some office in Manhattan?" He whipped the ball at me and it landed in my glove with a pop. "You need to wake up," he said. "Don't blow this."

Talking to Jim, I realized part of my problem was that I didn't have anyone to talk to. He could give me pep talks, but I didn't know anybody who was involved in the space program. I didn't even know anyone who knew anyone who was involved in the space program. I figured I should go to grad school, but what should I study there? What did I need to learn?

I decided to write a letter to NASA. I had no idea who to send it to, so I sent it to the top guy, NASA administrator James Beggs. He didn't write back, but I did get a reply from a man named Frank Coy, Beggs's executive officer. I guess he's the guy who got the overflow mail like my letter. For some reason he wrote back and said to give him a call. I did. He told me about different jobs at NASA and the different aerospace contractors. The upshot of the conversation was that no matter what I did, if I wanted to have any chance of being an astronaut, I had to go to graduate school.

Even though MIT had accepted me, I still had a hard time seeing myself there. I think my single biggest problem was that part of me believed I was supposed to be on that train to work every day. Even when I was at Columbia, I was a kid who thought I'd live on Long Island for the rest of my life. I was going to hang out with the same guys, watch every single Mets game, and be content with that life. In some ways, part of me still is that guy. But there was also the other part of me, the kid who walked out on his front lawn and looked up at the moon and dreamed of going there. I realized much later in life that the reason this decision between MIT and IBM was so agonizing was because it wasn't really about choosing a career; it was about deciding who I was, which part of myself I wanted to be, and that's the hardest decision any of us has to make.

I took a day off from work and drove up to visit MIT. I talked to some students and professors who were designing equipment and experiments to be used on the space shuttle. They were researching how the human body functioned in space, how to control robots on other planets. Once I saw that, I knew MIT was where I had to be. How I would pay for it, where Carola and I would end up, I had no idea. But I knew in my heart I had to at least give it my best shot.

If I had any remaining doubts about grad school, they disappeared the morning of January 28, 1986. I was at my desk and a coworker came by and said, "Mike, did you hear? The shuttle exploded." Somebody turned on a television in the reception area and we rushed in to watch. It was on every channel, playing over and over again: The space shuttle *Challenger* had exploded in this giant ball of flames, the debris flying off in a Y-shaped trail of smoke. The O-ring in the right solid rocket booster had failed, leaking burning-hot gas that had caused the explosion.

Seven crew members were on board: five astronauts, Dick Scobee, Michael Smith, Ron McNair, Ellison Onizuka, and Judy Resnik; Greg Jarvis, a payload specialist; and Christa McAuliffe, a schoolteacher chosen to be the first teacher in space.

All shuttle flights were suspended, and would be for the next two and a half years. I was going off to grad school to try to be an astronaut, and the whole space program was more or less on hold. But that didn't matter to me. It was strange, but after two years of wavering, once the accident happened, I never second-guessed myself. When the *Challenger* exploded, the world stood still. The president came on TV. Everybody paid attention. It reminded me how important the space program is.

I knew right then that I wanted to be a part of something that meaningful. I wanted to have something I was so passionate about that I'd be willing to risk everything for it. I wanted to know that if I ever got killed, I got killed doing something worthwhile. The kid who looked up at the moon and wasn't afraid to dream—I decided that part of me deserved a chance. I sat there in the reception area, watching the crash footage play over and over again on the television, and that was when it hit home for me: You only have one life. You have to spend it doing something that matters.

PART 2

MAYBE YOU'RE NOT
CUT OUT FOR THIS

4

THE SMART-KID OLYMPICS

MIT may be the most intimidating place on Earth. I felt like I was out of my league the day I showed up. The grad students you find at MIT are the ones who kick themselves because they "only" got a 790 out of 800 on their math GRE. I did not have a 790 math on my GRE. Nowhere close. And it's not just the smartest American kids. MIT draws brilliant people from all over the world. It's the best of the best from Algeria, from Thailand, from Brazil, from Poland. It's the smart-kid Olympics.

Then there was me: the guy from Long Island who filled out his application wrong.

What helped me to find my place at MIT was the same thing that helped push me toward Columbia: Somebody saw something in me. Once I'd decided on grad school, I started going to the New York Public Library on my IBM lunch breaks to learn what MIT was doing with the space program. I started reading about Professor Tom Sheridan, who was doing important work with human factors and robotics.

Human factors is fascinating to me; it's what drew me into studying industrial engineering at Columbia. Anytime you get in your car and you can work the brakes and the steering wheel and read the speedometer and not drive off the road in confusion, that's because an engineer who understands human factors designed it for you. There's the engineering side of it, which is designing and building the machines, but there's also the human operator side of it, which is understanding how the brain responds to different stimuli and how to account for that in your designs.

Tom Sheridan was a professor of mechanical engineering and a professor of applied psychology, and he was like a rock star in the world of human factors. He was also doing cutting-edge work with the space program, designing control systems for telerobotics—how an operator on Earth can accurately manipulate machines and systems on satellites or the space station or even other planets. He also seemed like a cool guy, a good man.

I made an appointment to go up to Cambridge and visit him. His office was cluttered with piles of books and papers everywhere, a bicycle stashed in the corner. He was a bit of an absentminded-professor type, sort of gray-haired and disheveled. But he was warm and friendly and down-to-earth, a thoughtful, caring person among the crazy hard-driving personalities at MIT; he kept a big poster on his wall with a photo of the Earth that said LOVE YOUR MOTHER. When we talked, he said he liked the fact that I was an industrial engineer, because it had given me some practical experience with human factors, something that most of the *Good Will Hunting* geniuses on campus didn't necessarily have. He told me if I came to MIT, he'd love to have me in his lab.

Life is funny. I'd applied to the wrong graduate program, but that eventually led me to the right one. I'd taken what I thought was the wrong undergraduate major, and it was the thing that set me apart and allowed me to find my niche. I don't know if there are any lessons to take from this except to realize that the things you think are mistakes may turn out not to be mistakes. I realized that wherever you are, if you make the most of what you've got, you can find a way to keep moving forward. The best advice I have for students is to follow your interests and study what you want to learn, and your career path will become clear. I packed up my office at IBM on July 4, 1986, and I moved to Cambridge, Massachusetts: the first stop, I hoped, on the road to space.

For the next six years, I had my head buried in books. That first semester was stressful, but incredible. I got a

half-time teaching assistantship that covered half my
tuition and gave me a small stipend. I was taking three
classes: Tom Sheridan's class, which was a project class;
a technology and policy proseminar; and an economics
class. It was tough, but I did well: two As and a B. Then,
the second semester, it got tougher. I took my first aerospace class, a satellite engineering class taught by Professor Walter Hollister, a short guy with a gigantic mustache,
who had flown fighter planes in Vietnam and became a
PhD in aeronautics and astronautics. (A fighter pilot *and*
a professor—how much cooler could you be?) The first
exam was brutal. When the test came back, I got a 35,
the lowest grade in the class. Mark Stephenson was a
buddy of mine, a really sharp army guy from West Point.
He walked up to me after the test and he said, "How'd
you do?"

I said, "I'm toast."

I told him about my 35. He had done better than me,
but not by a whole lot. We ended up talking to another
student, Wasif, who got a 38. Wasif was Indian but he'd
grown up in Scotland, so he had this thick Scottish accent. We started commiserating about our grades and how
tough it was at MIT. It was a relief to find out I wasn't the
only one struggling. I ended up forming a study group
with some students to help each other out. We'd stay up
late, ordering pizza, doing problem sets together, and
going over the notes night after night after night.

At the end of my first year, I went back to New York for a few weeks. Carola and I got engaged, but we decided not to get married for a couple of years, and she stayed in New York. I wanted to get some real experience with the space program that summer, so I wrote to Frank Coy again, inquiring about a summer job at NASA headquarters in DC. I wanted to get a general introduction to the space program, and headquarters seemed the best place to do that. I applied for and got a position cataloging the human factors work NASA was doing and compiling the information in a report for the NASA administrator.

I spent that summer in DC drinking everything in. NASA headquarters is close to the National Air and Space Museum. I'd go on my lunch breaks to walk around the museum. They had a brand-new IMAX theater, which was showing *The Dream Is Alive,* the first IMAX film shot aboard the space shuttle. I think I went to see that movie at least fifteen times. But the most valuable thing I did was meet people. I met *everyone.* I'm sure I was the youngest person in the building by a good fifteen years, so I stood out to begin with, and I made a point of shaking hands with and talking to every single person I could.

People could see my excitement, and with me being an engineering student, they knew I had potential. My dream didn't feel so crazy anymore, but the reality was sometimes surreal. One afternoon I walked into the cafeteria and Mike Collins was there having lunch; he was in town for a meeting, to discuss a possible mission to Mars, where I'd seen him earlier that day. Here was one of the *Apollo 11* astronauts, a guy I'd read about and idolized for years, and he was sitting at a table, eating by himself. I was beyond intimidated, but I knew if I didn't approach him, I would regret it for the rest of my life. I took a deep breath and walked over and asked if I could join him. "Sure," he said, "have a seat." He asked me who I was, what I did. I told him I was an engineering student at MIT, that I wanted to be an astronaut. He was friendly, chatted with me a while, asked what I was doing in school. I asked him if he had any advice. He told me if I was serious, I should look into working at one of the NASA space flight centers in Houston or Huntsville instead of headquarters in Washington, which turned out to be useful information.

The more I talked to people like Mike Collins, the more I realized that they were once the same guy I was: a young person with an impossible dream. Two years earlier I'd been clueless, lost, watching a grainy VHS tape of *The Right Stuff*. Now, here I was, having lunch with one of my childhood heroes, and we were just having a conversation. He didn't talk to me as if I was some delusional idiot who was wasting his time. He talked to me like I was someone who was supposed to be there at NASA. That alone was worth the whole summer in DC.

It got even tougher my second year. I decided to try to get two master's degrees at the same time; on top of the technology and policy degree, I was going for a master's in straight mechanical engineering, which I knew I'd need for the work I wanted to do with NASA and the astronaut program. Fall semester, I had four incredibly tough classes. I took dynamics from Stephen Crandall, who wrote the book on dynamics. I took mathematical principles for engineers from Gilbert Strang, who wrote the book on mathematical principles for engineers. The education I got was incredible, and not just the one in the classroom. I remember Tom Sheridan telling me once, "If you can learn to live with indignities in life, you can go far." And he's right. You can learn a lot by getting knocked down, and I got knocked down over and over again. And every time, I got up and kept going. I know there were students in my class who were smarter than me, but I don't know if there was anybody who worked harder than me.

In the spring of 1988, I graduated from MIT with two master's degrees: a master's of science in mechanical engineering and a master's of science in technology and policy. Now it was time for my next great challenge: driving to Alabama. I'd more or less begged my way into a fellowship from the NASA Graduate Student Researchers Program at the Marshall Space Flight Center in Huntsville. At the time, I was driving this 1976 Ford Grenada—the Ford Disaster, I called it. My car could barely make it around the block, let alone all the way to the Deep South. It had been in a flood, and the floor was rotted out; my father and I had to nail roofing shingles to the underside of the car to cover the holes. I loaded it up and prayed I didn't break down in the backwoods of Appalachia along the way.

I made it—barely. I found a cheap place to live and went to work in the Human Systems Integration Branch. My summer in Huntsville was pure fun. I assisted with some very cool robotics work. I was on a softball team. I met a lot of people my age, and we took road trips to Atlanta and Tennessee. In my free time I started building out my résumé with the kinds of things people told me I needed to be a good candidate for the astronaut program. I got scuba certified. That was challenging; I still wasn't a good swimmer. I started taking flying lessons to get my private pilot's license, and I ended up soloing a plane by the end of the summer.

After two years at MIT and two stints with NASA, I felt I was plugged into what was going on in the space program, not stumbling around in the dark. As I packed up my Ford Disaster and drove home from Alabama, there was only one cloud on the horizon, something I knew I had to go through but I'd been doing my best not to think about: my PhD.

5

FORCE FEEDBACK

One difficulty of becoming an astronaut is that no one can tell you how to become an astronaut. Even the people at NASA can't tell you how to become an astronaut, because the chances of actually becoming an astronaut are so small. Everyone is encouraging, but no one has any ironclad advice. I could get five PhDs and still never be an astronaut, and not every astronaut has a PhD. The advice I got was "You should get the PhD because you want the PhD, because having that degree will make you happy in and of itself, and the astronaut dream may happen or it may not."

Getting my master's from MIT had nearly killed me, and I knew going for a PhD would be worse. I'd been accepted to the doctoral program; back then, if you completed your master's, MIT would let you go for a PhD almost automatically. But I was on the fence about it.

Is this really how I want to spend the next four years of my life?

At that point I didn't have anything on my résumé that would give me a leg up over anyone else. I was never in the military; I wasn't an ace test pilot; my academic credentials were solid but nothing out of the ordinary. Ultimately, I decided that a PhD from MIT was not only my best chance of setting myself apart, it was also a remarkable opportunity I couldn't pass up.

Once I decided to go for my PhD, I had to figure out what my thesis would be. I knew I didn't want to do straight mechanical engineering. I wanted to be able to incorporate some of the work on human factors that I'd been doing with Tom Sheridan. What I was interested in was robotics and control systems: how robots interface with human operators and, more specifically, how they do it in space.

Whenever you manipulate an object with your hand, pulling a lever or twisting a knob, the amount of resistance it gives you is something you can feel. It's instantaneous, and you can react to it right away. The brain knows automatically how to read those signals and adjust to apply more force or less. But if you're manipulating an object remotely via a robot—for example, communicating with a rover on Mars—there's a time delay between the signals the robot is sending to you and the commands you're sending to it. You might push too hard or not hard enough, based on wrong information about what's happening on the other end, and the object you're manipulating becomes unstable very quickly and you start knocking into things. It's a problem of force information, force feedback.

At that time, the way robot designers dealt with this issue was by having a display for human operators that showed the levels of force feedback visually, like a speedometer that ratchets up or down. The problem was that operators already needed to have their eyes on the video feed of the object they were manipulating; having another screen to look at didn't exactly make things any easier. My idea was that you could eliminate that screen and transmit the necessary force feedback through an operator's other senses: touch and hearing. A slight vibration on your skin or a sound in your ear would indicate the level and direction of force feedback, allowing you to respond accordingly.

Pretty cool, right?

Tom Sheridan agreed to be my advisor, and I approached three other professors to serve on my thesis committee: Richard Held, a brain and cognitive science professor who was an expert on physiology and the human senses; Dave Akin, an aeronautics and astronautics professor who specialized in aerospace systems and space robotics; and Nat Durlach, an electrical engineering research scientist who worked with electronics and human perception.

As a PhD candidate, I had to pass a qualifying exam. It included written and oral components that tested basic engineering concepts and a presentation of where I was with my research. It was a way of making sure I was on track to successfully complete my work and also to make sure my engineering knowledge was up to MIT PhD standards: "Quality control," Sheridan used to call it. Basically, they didn't want me hanging around, wasting my time, if I was not going to be successful.

Some PhD candidates take their qualifier about six months in. I figured I'd need at least a year to prepare, so I scheduled my exam for the summer after my first PhD year and got to work.

That whole year was difficult. One of the only bright spots was that the shuttle had started flying again. On September 29, 1988, STS-26, the first flight since *Challenger,* launched from Kennedy Space Center for a successful four-day mission aboard space shuttle *Discovery,* which meant the space program was back in full swing and there would be more astronaut jobs in the future. I'd sent away for an application to be an astronaut and was working on it here and there. I didn't expect to get in; I knew most people got rejected on their first try. But I wanted to get my name in the hopper anyway.

Other than that, it was a gloomy time for me. Most of my good friends left after finishing their master's degrees. I was working alone, living alone. I'd wake up, trudge through the Boston winter to go sit in a carrel in the library, study all day, work in the lab, and go home to the empty dorm. Looming over me the whole time was this dreaded qualifying exam. I studied and studied and studied, but I really had no idea what I was doing. I had no idea if I was studying the right material the right way. I'd never faced anything like this. I was just cramming information into my head and hoping for the best.

D-day finally came the week of June 22, 1989. That same week, the Mets traded my favorite player, Roger McDowell, and future MVP Lenny Dykstra to the Phillies, one of the worst trades of all time. I took it as a bad omen. It was. The day of the oral exam and research presentation, I woke up terrified. I walked over to Professor Sheridan's office, dreading what was to come. Sheridan and the rest of my committee were lined up in chairs around a coffee table and then there was me, alone, standing at a chalkboard in front of them with nothing but a piece of chalk in my hand to show my work and defend myself.

I needed more than a piece of chalk to save me that day. An oral exam can be like a firing squad. It's their job to tear you apart, challenge your assumptions, force you to defend your conclusions. If they find a weakness in your work, they'll home in on it and take you down. Albert Einstein could be up there and they'd tear him to shreds, too.

I won't keep you in suspense: It was a massacre. They

were bombarding me with questions from every angle. Why this? What's your evidence for that? I was stumbling through my answers, losing my train of thought, trying to go back and start over. After a certain point, I was completely lost. They could have asked me "What's two plus two?" and I don't think I could have given them a clear answer.

I walked out of that room completely traumatized. I wandered around the campus in a daze. I'd blown my PhD. I'd blown everything. My NASA application was sitting at home on my desk, filled out and ready to submit. Now what was the point in that? Carola and I were getting married in a few weeks. She was already packing up and planning to move to Boston. We had a place picked out, this great one-bedroom by Harvard Square with a big bay window looking out on Massachusetts Avenue. Now that whole future had crumbled. What was I going to tell her?

I went back to Sheridan's office a couple of hours later. When he opened the door, I could tell by his expression that the results weren't good. "I didn't pass, did I?"

He looked away, shook his head, and said, "No, Mike. You didn't pass."

Sheridan truly cared about his students; it wasn't easy for him to deliver that news, but he had to do it.

I had the option, if I wanted it, of coming back and taking the exam again in six months. But I'd failed so utterly and completely that he said to me, point-blank, "You should think about whether or not it's worth your time to do that." Sheridan had always been so supportive, a wonderful man. Without him I wouldn't have made it as far as I did. But here he was telling me, in so many words: *Maybe you're not cut out for this.* Hearing someone who had been so encouraging be so brutally candid now was difficult to take. I sat there in his office, completely and totally demoralized. A year earlier I'd been walking on air: working at NASA, meeting my childhood heroes. Now everything had come crashing back to earth, and I had no idea how to get back up.

When I got home from blowing my qualifying exam, my completed NASA application sitting on my desk was like salt in my wound. My first thought was *Well, that's done.* Then I thought about it and decided to send it in anyway. I'd failed the test, but they were offering me another crack at it, and until I decided what to do, I was still a PhD candidate at MIT, and many astronauts with only a master's degree do get picked. So I mailed it off without telling them *Hey, and by the way, I just failed my PhD qualifying exam!* I figured by the time anybody looked at the application, I'd have another crack at the test, if I felt it was worth taking it again. I was all but sure it wasn't.

Then I went back to Huntsville. I owed them three more weeks of work for my graduate fellowship. The summer before, I'd been excited, confident. Now I was totally down in the dumps. The three weeks I was there happened to coincide with a celebration for the twentieth anniversary of the moon landing—twenty years since I'd stood out on my lawn and looked up at the moon and dreamed about going there someday. They were having lectures and symposiums, and all the *Apollo* astronauts were coming through to give talks and be recognized. Neil Armstrong was there. Buzz Aldrin and Mike Collins and Pete Conrad were there. But instead of being inspired, I was more like *Great, this will never be me. I'm never going to be one of these guys.*

One of the Apollo astronauts there that week was Charlie Duke, who flew with John Young on *Apollo 16*. He was also one of the four moonwalkers who came through MIT. I attended the talk that he gave, and after it was over, he was signing autographs. I picked up an Apollo postcard and got in line to go up to the table where he was sitting. While he signed the postcard for me, he said, "So what do you do?"

I said, "I'm a research fellow here in Huntsville, and I'm a student at MIT."

He said, "MIT? Man, that place kicked my butt. I never thought I'd make it out of there, but somehow I did."

I stood there, thinking, *Wow. This guy walked on the moon, and even* he *barely made it out of MIT. And he might never have made it to the moon if he hadn't made it out of*

MIT. Charlie Duke and the other Apollo astronauts, before they walked on the moon, had all walked a mile in my
shoes. The journey to space wasn't easy, but if I gave up,
it would be over.

In that moment, I learned how much power astronauts
have to inspire people. I walked away from the table and I
knew: I had to go back. I had to try again. Maybe I wasn't
a failure. Maybe a PhD from MIT is something that's really
hard and it knocks everyone down and forces them to get
back up. And this wasn't only my PhD at stake; my whole
space dream was on the line. I decided that, as bad as I
went down in flames the first time, I had to turn it around
and take the test again. If I didn't at least try, I'd always
look back and be disappointed with myself, and wonder
What if?

6

HUMAN FACTORS

That fall, after Carola and I were married over the summer in New York, and while she and I were unpacking boxes in our apartment on Massachusetts Avenue, I got a call from a flight surgeon at NASA with a question about my application. I knew right away why he was calling.

"Hey, what's the deal with your eyes?" he asked.

This was the moment I'd been trying to avoid. On the astronaut application, there's a box where you're supposed to put your eyesight down if you know it. I'd left the box blank, thinking they'd see it and go, *Oh, maybe he's never had his eyes checked, so he must see fine.* But the reason I'd left it blank is because I'd had them checked, many times, and I knew they were bad.

I'd known since seventh grade when I was in the stands at a Mets game trying to write down the lineup on my scorecard, and I couldn't read the scoreboard across the field. I got glasses, but I hated them, so I didn't use them that much. I tried wearing them while playing in a baseball game once, and I took a line drive in the face that broke my nose. After that, I went around nearly blind most of the time. By eleventh grade, my eyes were bad enough that I had to squint to see the basket on the basketball court. I started wearing contact lenses, and from then on, I was fine. Until NASA called.

Back then, having good uncorrected eyesight was required for becoming an astronaut. It was a deal breaker. If you didn't make the cutoff, that was it. Done. Finished. You're out. Luckily, times now have changed in that regard. For those aspiring astronauts without good vision, have no fear. A few years ago NASA realized that the vision requirements were outdated, they have been relaxed. The requirements that had me disqualified no longer exist. Today there would be no issue medically with my vision. But back in 1989, it was disqualifying. Progress often comes too late. The flight surgeon didn't know I'd skipped the question. He thought I'd missed the box. I fished out one of my old prescription slips and told him what it was. He said, "Yeah, that's no good. We don't need 20/20, but we do need at least 20/200. We can't take you."

I said, "Is there anything I can do?"

"There is this one procedure you can try," he told me. "It's called orthokeratology. Check it out. Maybe you can give that a shot and resubmit another application if you can get your eyes better. But based on what we have now, I'll have to reject you."

Then, as we were getting off the phone, he said, "Look, if your application got to me, that means you're in the highly qualified section of candidates. You're in the top 10 percent, and you should feel good about making it this far. If you can get your eyes fixed, you've got a real chance."

When I hung up, I was in shock: the top 10 percent! That was all the motivation I needed to keep going. I wasn't even that upset about the eye problem. It was another obstacle I had to deal with, but maybe I could fix it. I was ready to take on anything if I was that close to making my dream come true.

I did some research and I learned that orthokeratology is a process where hard contact lenses are used to reshape the eye. When doctors first started prescribing contacts to people back in the 1940s, the first lenses they invented weren't the nice, soft ones we have today; they were pieces of hard glass or plastic. Doctors noticed that, after wearing these hard lenses for a while, people would wake up and see without any assistance.

What these hard lenses would do was reshape a patient's cornea—they'd flatten your eyeball, basically refocusing the light onto the retina—improving the patient's vision. The problem was that, once you took the lenses out, after a couple of days your eyes would go back to their normal shape. The eye tissue pops back to its natural resting place. But supposedly, if you stuck with it, you could improve your unaided vision for a period of time.

I decided to give it a shot. I found a Boston doctor who specialized in orthokeratology. He prescribed hard lenses for me, and my vision started getting better. It would stay better for a couple of days after I took the lenses out. After a few months, my vision fell within the standard for the astronaut program and I was ready to submit another application. Surely, NASA would want me now. All I had to do was go back to MIT and do the impossible thing that had nearly killed me: pass my qualifying exam.

Classes started up again at the beginning of September. My next crack at the qualifier was scheduled for the end of November. I had three months to turn everything around.

I took statistics, and I made a buddy in that class, Roger Alexander from Trinidad. We bonded quickly because we both fell into the hardworking-regular-guy category at MIT and not the eccentric-supergenius category. Roger lived in one of the graduate dorms, in an apartment with four guys sharing a kitchen and a common area. We'd study there in the evenings. I'll never forget one night when we had a problem set that was killing us. We couldn't crack it, and then, around two in the morning, Roger's roommate, Greg Chamitoff, wandered out into the common area in his gym shorts, eating this gigantic orange. Chamitoff was one freakishly smart dude. You could tell there was a lot of power in his brain. MIT's mascot is the beaver, because the beaver is the engineer of nature. Not coincidentally, it also does most of its work at night. Chamitoff fit the description cold. I never saw him much during daylight hours. He walked over to us, looking like he'd just woken up, and said, "What are you guys doing?" We told him this problem had us stumped. He asked if he could see the textbook, and we showed it to him. He looked it over for about a minute or so and said, "Yeah. Do this and this and this, and you got it." We'd been staring at this problem all night, and Greg solved the whole thing in his head in a few seconds, standing there in his shorts, slurping orange juice off his fingers.

Greg wanted to become an astronaut, too. At that point he'd already passed his PhD qualifying exam. We started talking. He told me what he did to prepare was to practice the oral exam with his friends. They would grill each other as if they were each other's thesis committee, because passing the exam wasn't just about knowing the information—it was about being able to anticipate the questions and think on your feet without getting rattled. Greg offered to do the same for me: assemble a practice committee of guys who'd passed their qualifiers, who knew what the drill was. They'd put me through the paces and toughen me up.

The mistake I made with my PhD to that point was that I forgot to find a team. I thought I was running a marathon by myself, and that's how I'd trained for it. I took Greg up on his offer to run the mock oral exams. Every week, my fellow students would grill me. Nick Patrick, a British guy who also wanted to be an astronaut, helped a great deal. So did two other guys, Cliff Federspiel and Mohammed Yahiaoui. They were merciless. Every week, I'd stand up there alone at the blackboard with my little piece of chalk and they'd tear me to shreds. They made me rethink the weak assumptions I'd put into my work. They made me learn how to think on the fly and express my ideas clearly. They'd pound me and pound me and pound me.

What amazed me was that Greg and the other guys didn't have to help me. They were carrying full doctoral course loads, too, and they'd already passed their qualifiers, so it's not like I was doing anything to help them in return. But they did it anyway. Because that's what you're supposed to do. That's how a team works. You help the people around you, and everybody's better off for it. The crazy thing is that some of those guys also wanted to be astronauts, too, but they never saw it as a competition. We were on the same team, where you want everyone around you to be as successful as possible, because in some way or another, their success will become your success. It's good karma—what goes around comes around.

When Thanksgiving week rolled around, it was time for me to face the real firing squad again. On Wednesday morning I went back down to Professor Sheridan's office. It was the same setup as before, my advisors seated around the coffee table, me with my little piece of chalk standing in front of the chalkboard. They got settled in and went to work on me.

They hit me with a ton of tough questions in a row. *Bam, bam, bam,* switching back and forth from control systems to spacecraft systems to neuroscience, jumping around to try to trip me up. Then they came after me on my research. The first time I went in, my research wasn't solid. Now, thanks to my weekly grilling from Greg and his crew, I'd thrown out my weak ideas and assumptions. My work stood up and I was able to defend it. The whole experience was every bit as brutal as before. I didn't breeze through it, by any means, but I wasn't stumbling and stuttering through my answers. I stayed calm and focused and on my game for the whole two hours.

When it was over, they asked me to leave the room so they could decide my fate. I stepped out and closed the door behind me. Then, quietly, I turned and put my ear to the door to try to hear what they were saying. I heard one of them say, "Well, he's obviously got a lot of ability, but . . ."

When I heard that "but," I turned and walked away. I left the building and walked around campus and tried to ignore the questions racing through my mind. Did I pass? Did I fail? Am I staying? Am I going? Am I going to have a good Thanksgiving or a bad Thanksgiving? Whatever happened in that room was going to alter the course of the rest of my life.

I knew, walking around, there was still a decent chance that I'd failed. Weird as it sounds, I was ready to fail this time. I'd failed the first go-round because I wasn't prepared and had made a bunch of stupid mistakes. That, I couldn't live with. But if I failed this time, at least I'd know I went down swinging and giving it everything I had. If you're going to fail, that's how you want to do it.

After a half hour, I went back to Sheridan's office to get the news. They started off with this long list of things I needed to work on. You did well on this, but you need to work on that, all very vague. I was good in control systems, Sheridan said, but I needed help in basic engineering concepts. Then one of them said maybe I should be a teaching assistant, that teaching undergrads would help me work on the areas where I needed help. That set off this whole discussion. And on and on.

Eventually, I jumped in and said, "Um, can I ask a question? I'm going home for Thanksgiving tomorrow, and my mother is going to ask me if I passed my qualifying exam. What do I tell her?"

Sheridan stopped and gave me this look. He said, "Oh.

No, no. Yeah, you passed. We're just trying to figure out what you need to do next."

That was all I needed to know. The rest of the conversation, I nodded and smiled and said yes to everything. I told them I would teach whatever they wanted me to teach, I would take whatever they wanted me to take. I didn't care: I'd *passed.*

7

DISQUALIFIED

At 10:00 P.M. on March 16, 1993, Carola gave birth to our beautiful baby girl, Gabby. We took her home and it was like a light had come into my life. Everything seemed better.

Gabby was born in Houston. Eight months earlier, after finishing my PhD, I'd taken a huge leap and moved to Texas for a job with McDonnell Douglas, the aerospace contractor. The chance of my becoming an astronaut was still the longest of long shots; I'd applied to the program a second time in the summer of 1991 and been rejected again. But I believed that being a part of the space community in Houston, where I could be close to the space program and get to know the people involved, was the best chance I had. I reached out to former astronaut Bob Overmyer at McDonnell Douglas, and the company made me an offer to head up their independent research and development team for robotics. My job would be to think up new ways to use robots in space. On August 19, 1992—my thirtieth birthday, as it turned out—my newly pregnant wife and I packed up our apartment in Boston and started a new life. In Texas.

We bought a house in Clear Lake, the suburb southwest of Houston where the Johnson Space Center is located. After a lifetime in the Northeast, it was a rough adjustment, but we'd stumbled into a wonderful community and we slowly got acclimated. Clear Lake is a company town. Nearly everyone is tied to NASA and the aerospace industry in some way or another. Our neighborhood was right off Space Center Boulevard, about five minutes from the entrance to the Johnson Space Center. It was like living in Astronautville. My whole life these guys were my heroes. Now they were my neighbors.

Steve Smith became an astronaut with the class of '92 and was on his way to becoming one of the top spacewalkers in NASA history. Steve is one of those people who's always in a good mood, has a huge smile, is friendly to everyone. He was so generous, there were times I thought he wasn't human. He was also tall and impossibly fit. Those barbells at the end of the rack that are covered with dust because nobody at the gym uses them? Steve would go right for them. He was an All-American water polo player at Stanford and captain of the 1980 NCAA Championship team. He's one of those guys who's phenomenal at everything—but you can't hate him for it because he's also the nicest guy you've ever met. Steve lived right around the corner and had a daughter about Gabby's age. He became a close friend, mentor, and confidant.

I started running into astronauts everywhere I went, even at our church, St. Clare of Assisi Catholic Church, which was so new it didn't have a building yet. While it was being built, they held Mass in a storefront in a strip mall next to a hardware store. I called it St. Clare of the Shopping Mall. Kevin Kregel and his family went to St. Clare with us. He was a fighter pilot out of the Air Force Academy who did an exchange with the Navy to attend the Navy Test Pilot School. Better than that: Kevin was from Long Island. The first time we met, he'd heard me speaking and walked up to me with a raised eyebrow. "You ever go to Solomon Grundy's?" My eyes lit up. Solomon Grundy's was a rock club on Long Island in the eighties; I loved the place.

"Yeah," I said. "You from around there?"

"Yup," he said. "I placed you right away with the accent." Kevin was a bit older than me, but he could easily have been one of the guys on my old Police Boys Club baseball team. Knowing that someone who grew up minutes away from where I did had become an astronaut was a huge inspiration.

Working at McDonnell Douglas, I was back in the sea

of desks and cubicles again, just like at Sperry and IBM. Only now I was in a different world. I was right down the road from the Johnson Space Center and Ellington Field. I can still remember my first Saturday living in Clear Lake. The Texas Air National Guard flies F-16s out of Ellington, and one of them came screaming overhead. Most homeowners wouldn't care for that, but I thought it was awesome. I was that much closer to where I wanted to be, and it made everything worthwhile.

As for the job itself, I wasn't sure I'd like it at first, but in the end, it turned out to be a wonderful opportunity. For my research project, I felt I needed one good idea, something big to sink my teeth into that could make a contribution. I wanted to design and build something that NASA needed, something that would help human spaceflight. I convinced the robotics instructors at the Johnson Space Center to let me go through some robotics training and work with some real astronauts who could help me understand how the shuttle's robotic tools could be improved. One afternoon in the spring of '93, right around the time Gabby was born, I was standing up on a simulator platform, where some astronauts were training to "fly" the shuttle's robot arm. The arm's official name was the remote manipulator system, or the RMS. Since it was made in Canada, we also called it the Canadarm. It was a giant crane used to move objects around outside the shuttle, like satellites or space station modules. It was also used to position spacewalkers to perform their tasks; they would ride on the front of the arm in a foot restraint. In the microgravity of space, the arm can manipulate something with the size and mass of a school bus.

The arm was controlled by astronauts inside the shuttle while they looked outside, into the payload bay of the orbiter, through the aft flight deck windows. They manipulated it via two hand controllers: a left-handed one for translations (XYZ motions), and a right-handed one for rotations (roll, pitch, and yaw motions). Flying the arm required a fair amount of training and skill and was one of the major jobs an astronaut performed on the space shuttle.

As I observed this simulation, I noticed they were using cameras to track the arm's movement, but they didn't always have a clear view with the camera, so they were looking at digital readouts to get the arm's XYZ coordinates or its pitch, yaw, and roll. Then they were taking that data and figuring out what they needed to do on the fly. It was an incredibly convoluted and counterintuitive way to manipulate this arm. It was similar to the sensory feedback issue I'd dealt with at MIT. The control system for this robot arm needed better human factors.

I realized that the solution, what they needed, was a visual display that rendered the data graphically in real time, like a video game. There was another engineer at McDonnell Douglas at the time, Jack Brazzell, who had

figured out a way to help with shuttle rendezvous by getting data to display graphically through a software interface on a laptop computer. Laptops changed everything.
They allowed astronauts and developers to make some
forward-thinking innovations because now they were
free to experiment and try new things. I started working with Jack, piggybacking on some of the work he had
done on his laptop rendezvous display, getting his advice
on how to get my project on board the shuttle. I found a
couple of great programmers, Albert Rodriguez and Mike
Meschler, and I brought them on my team to help me create this laptop video game interface to improve control of
the robot arm.

Within a few months, we had a working demo, and
then, much to my surprise, I found my sales experience at
IBM coming into play. Because now I had to sell my idea. I
had to demonstrate to astronauts and others at NASA the
benefits of the new system. If you want NASA to adopt
something you've built and incorporate it into their program, you need people—astronauts, especially—to get
behind you and tell the decision makers, "Hey, we want
this. We need this."

McDonnell Douglas had strong relationships with the
astronaut office already in place, and I used those to start
knocking on doors. I demonstrated my display system to
whoever would listen. I got some polite rejections from a
few people who didn't get it, but I finally connected with

a Swiss astronaut named Claude Nicollier, the chief of the Astronaut Office Robotics Branch. Claude was a former fighter pilot, tall and thin, warm and gracious, and quick to make a joke. He spoke perfect English with a slight, very elegant accent. The first time I met him, I was getting my display hooked up to a simulator. Claude walked in eating a vanilla ice-cream cone. He stood there quietly eating the ice cream and watched me try the display. "I like what you have," he said. "We should talk more." He sounded like a Swiss James Bond.

Claude started talking up my idea, and people started to take notice. Jan Davis and Ellen Ochoa, who worked with Claude in the robotics branch, both loved the display and started helping me design and implement it. Jan was from Huntsville, warm and friendly and down-to-earth. She grew up in the shadow of the Marshall Space Flight Center and, like me, had dreamed of going to space for as long as she could remember. She'd actually gone to the launch of *Apollo 11* and made a sign that said, LOOK OUT, MOON. HERE COMES HUNTSVILLE.

Ellen Ochoa was soft-spoken, but she was so sharp and capable that she could command a room because everyone knew that her thoughts were valuable. To no one's surprise, she went on to become head of the Johnson Space Center.

Jan, Ellen, and Claude started pushing to get my robot-arm display flown and tested on a future shuttle mission, and together we made it happen. NASA eventually decided that my display would be flown and tested on STS-69 in June 1995. It was one of the proudest moments of my life to that point: Even if I never made it to space, something I'd created actually would.

Working with the people in the robotics branch the way I did made me thankful once again for my own dumb luck. If I'd had a clue what I was doing as an undergrad, I might have been a more traditional aero/astro guy and specialized in something like jet propulsion, and I'd have been off in a lab somewhere working with a bunch of machines every day. But I hadn't specialized in jet propulsion. I'd specialized in human factors, which meant I was working with the humans—the astronauts. In hindsight, it was one of the best calls I could have made. Because when it comes time to choose a new class of astronauts, for the most part the astronauts do the choosing. No politician in Washington has any say in who gets to fly in space. Astronauts make up the majority of the votes on the selection committee, and through my work, I was able to spend hours and hours getting to know them.

And I liked them. Every time I drove in to the Johnson Space Center, I had a voice in the back of my head telling me: *This is it. I want to be a part of this. I want this more than anything.*

•   •   •

The astronaut selection process takes almost a year. In the summer of '93, NASA started taking applications for the astronaut class of 1994. I submitted mine. Then there was a problem with funding and the class of '94 got scrapped. They held on to everyone's applications and told us they were going to wait a year and pick people for '95. A year ticked by, and the following summer, I updated my résumé and my recommendations, sent them in, and waited by the phone.

I was an old hand at this by now, no longer flying blind. I had people to talk to, and they showed me how the process works. One of them told me, "You do know you can see your file, right? You can request to see what they've got on you and what they've said about you in the past."

Smart idea. I requested my file and, sure enough, I saw a mistake I'd made, why my application might have hit a wall the second time. When I'd worked at NASA headquarters in the summer of '87, my supervisor was this guy who was a little aloof. We weren't close, but I'd put him down as a reference anyway because he was a big name. I did that with a couple of the recommendations: I picked people I thought were important instead of people who knew me. That was a mistake. This supervisor and I, we hadn't interacted much, and he'd checked off "average" or "don't know" to nearly every question. At one point he'd checked "Don't know, don't know, don't know" all the way down the page. The last question was open-ended: "What else can you tell us about this person?" He'd written in, "I just don't know."

So that was bad. I wasn't going to make that mistake again. I asked Ellen Ochoa to write me a letter of recommendation, and she did. At McDonnell Douglas, I had Bob Overmyer. He knew me well and wrote me a great recommendation. I had my PhD, I'd published several papers, I was building a robotics display for the shuttle. It had taken me ten years. Exactly one decade after walking out of *The Right Stuff* at the Floral Park theater, I'd put together an astronaut application about as strong as I was ever going to get.

On August 4, I got the call. It was a Thursday. I was sitting at my desk at work and the phone rang. A woman's voice said, "Hi, this is Teresa Gomez from the astronaut selection office. We're wondering if you would be interested in coming in to interview to be an astronaut candidate?"

"Yes," I said. I was practically jumping up and down.

She said, "Okay, this is a bit of short notice, but we have someone who canceled for next week, and we're trying to get someone local so we won't have to arrange travel. But if you can't make it next week, you can wait and come in week five or six."

"I'll come next week," I said. "I don't want to wait and take any chance that you'll change your mind."

Teresa had me come by the Johnson Space Center to pick up an information packet. I went home and read it, and it was fairly basic: where to be, how to dress, etc. Then I came to the part about the eye exam. It said, "You will be given a series of extensive eye exams. We ask that those of you who wear contact lenses do not wear them for two weeks leading up to the test." When I read that, I knew I was in trouble.

They insist on that because they want your eyes as close to their natural state as possible for the exam; contacts can cause edema, a swelling of the eye, and they want you to be completely free of that. But I was going in on short notice. I didn't have two weeks to let my eyes rest. And I was still using my orthokeratology lenses to flatten my eyeballs. I'd been wearing them for four years now. I knew if I took them out, within a couple of days I wouldn't be able to see very well. I called my eye doctor in Boston and he said, "Your lenses won't cause any edema. I wouldn't worry about it." So I thought about it and decided it would be okay for me to leave the contacts in.

NASA had two optometrists, Bob Gibson and Keith Manuel. Their job was to conduct the eye exams and report the results to the flight surgeons who made the final recommendations on medical fitness to the selection committee. Rainer Effenhauser was the flight surgeon overseeing my group of applicants, but Smith Johnston was another flight surgeon on staff I got to know, and he helped talk me through parts of the process as well. Keith Manuel was running the eye exams that day. He ended up being my neighbor, a great guy, but that day I walked in hating him. I knew the eye exam was the biggest thing between me and a clean bill of health, and I went in thinking of him as my nemesis.

The first thing Keith had me do was the standard eye chart to test my unaided acuity and to see if he could correct me to 20/20. He put me through the paces. "Read line one." "Read line two." He started using different lenses to try to correct me to 20/20, and he got frustrated. He couldn't do it. He said, "I don't know what the problem is. You're not seeing 20/20 no matter what I do here."

Then, to test my unaided acuity, he put me on the Landolt C machine. I'd never heard of it before, but it's way more sophisticated than the eye chart. It's a machine that flashes the letter "C" in front of you over and over again, randomly, in rapid succession, projected at different depths and with the open part of the "C" facing in different directions. It's fast. You can't sit there taking your time. You have a joystick and you have to move it up, down, right, or left in response to which way the "C" is facing.

The Landolt C is a very accurate vision test. Needless to say, I did not pass. It did not go well at all. I can't remember how many I missed; it might have been all of them. Finally, Keith said, "Okay, the last thing I have to do is map your eyeball." Map my eyeball? I didn't even know what that was. But basically, it's exactly what it sounds like. It's a machine that takes a 3-D topographical map of your eyeball; it's a way to determine the shape and health of your corneas. Keith hooked me up to this contraption and futzed with it for a few minutes. He said, "You've got a flat eyeball."

"That's from the orthokeratology," I said. "One of the flight surgeons recommended that to me as something I could do to improve my acuity."

"Yes," he explained, "but orthokeratology lenses are a special case. You were supposed to stop using them six months in advance to let your eyeball revert to its normal shape."

I hadn't known that. I wouldn't get the official results until later in the week, but I knew they'd be bad. Even worse, I still had the most important part of the week ahead of me: the interview. I had to sit down at a conference table with the entire astronaut selection committee. Some of the biggest names at NASA were on this board.

The interview went well. We had a friendly chat. They asked me about what it was like growing up on Long Island, my playing the trumpet in the school band, my dad being a fire inspector, random things. They asked a few questions about my work and my research, but mostly it was get-to-know-you type questions. I told a few funny stories, got a few laughs. We got so wrapped up in talking that the hour flew by. Finally, Steve Hawley, an astronaut, said, "Hey, we're out of time. Is there anything you want to add?"

I said, "Not really, just that I appreciate the opportunity. This has been the highlight of my life coming in here, and whatever happens, happens." We stood up and everyone shook my hand. Everybody was happy and smiling. I felt good about it. I felt like I belonged in that room. Those were my people. This was the team I was supposed to be on. But I knew that when I woke up the next morning, it was going to be the worst day of my life.

On Friday, August 12, 1994—before I even got to the news waiting for me at NASA—Major League Baseball went on strike. They'd played the last game of the season the night before, and then that morning the players of every single team walked out in protest over the salary cap. The rest of the season wound up canceled, and there would be no World Series for the first time since 1904. The strike was bitter and it was ugly and the whole future of the sport looked grim, much like my chances of being an astronaut. It was the mother of all bad omens.

On the drive over to the space center to meet with the flight surgeons and get my medical results, I was actually hoping for something else to be wrong other than my eyes. I was praying for something so far out of my control that I could throw my hands up and say, "Well, that's life.

Nothing I can do." No such luck. I had met and surpassed all the medical criteria for the job—except one.

I sat down with Rainer Effenhauser and he gave me the news about my eyes. "Your unaided acuity is beyond our limit," he said, "so we have to DQ you on that. We couldn't correct you to 20/20, either, so we have to DQ you on that. And you've got flat eyeballs in your head. We've got to DQ you on that, too. I'm sorry, but we can't take you. With these results, there isn't a chance you can be considered. You're medically disqualified."

The words hung there in the air: "medically disqualified." Not "underqualified" or "in need of more experience" but physically and genetically unfit for service. I was crushed. It'd been ten years. Ten years of my life I'd been working toward this goal. I didn't know whether to feel angry or sad or frustrated or what. My whole body was numb.

After I got the news, I called up Duane Ross, the head of the Astronaut Selection Office, and asked if I could come by and talk to him. I wanted to know if there was anything—*anything*—that I could do. Duane had been head of the selection office since the shuttle program began. He was the warmest, most gracious guy, the kind of guy you wanted in your corner because you knew he'd do whatever he could for you. He told me to come by and we sat down and he couldn't have been nicer. He said, "Mike, I want you to know we were all disappointed

when those results came back. I can't tell you we would
have picked you, but I can tell you that you were one of
the people we were talking about. Maybe you wouldn't
have gotten it this time, but you might have gotten it in a
future selection."

To hear him say that broke my heart: I was so close. It
was right there in front of me. I called some of the astronauts on the selection committee and asked them if they
minded giving me their feedback, too. They all took the
time to speak with me and not one of them said, "Hey,
this isn't worth your while. Good luck." If they had, I
think I might have given up. But they didn't. Every single one of them took me aside and told me, "You know,
if you can do anything about your eyes, you should give
it a try."

At that point I decided if I was going to be told no, I
wanted to be told no. I didn't want to be told, "We wish
we could have considered you." After everything I'd in-
vested, for me to walk away, the door had to be closed and
closed forever. As long as it was open, even just a crack, I
knew that I couldn't bring myself to stop trying. I'd made
it too far and come too close to give up, and I had nothing
left to lose. There was only one thing I had to do to get
back in the mix: I had to learn how to see better. I once
heard baseball legend Joe Torre say, "You can control your
effort, but you can't control the outcome." He was refer-
ring to sports, but I think that applies to many challenges

in life. I understood I could not control the outcome of my application. I could not force NASA to accept me into the astronaut program. But I could control my effort and continue to apply. I decided that as long as I was breathing, I would keep trying, right up to the end.

8

YES OR NO

Monday morning I was back at work at McDonnell Douglas and I ran into Bob Overmyer in the hall. He said, "What happened?"

"I got medically DQ'd."

"Your eyesight?" he said. "Yeah, that happens with a lot of people. I fought those tests for years." As a former military pilot and astronaut, Bob knew all about the eye test. For as long as there have been planes in the sky, pilots and astronauts have been running scared from the eye exam—because you can be the best, most qualified pilot in the world and then get benched for something that's 100 percent beyond your control.

Bob was actually encouraging. "This is only your first time," he said. "Don't give up. You'll get another shot and you may get back into the game." He told me pilots do all kinds of wacky things to try to beat the eye test. "You know what I used to do?" Bob said. "I'd dehydrate myself. I'd schedule the exam for Monday morning, and over the weekend I wouldn't drink anything. I'd run like crazy, get all the water out of my system. That way you dry out the eyeball and make it stiffer and it bends the light better."

"Okay," I said. "Makes sense. I'll give it a shot."

That same afternoon, I was at the Johnson Space Center and I saw Kevin Kregel in the hallway. I told him what had happened. He said, "Those eye tests will kill you every time. But you know what you gotta do, right?"

"What's that?"

"Drink lots of water. Drink as much water as you can, for days. The morning you go in, don't even pee. It'll make your eyeball more viscous and it'll bend the light better."

It actually made me feel better, knowing that I wasn't the only guy who'd been through this and nobody else had a clue what to do, either. Bob and Kevin had both faced the same obstacle and they'd overcome it and both had become astronauts. That gave me hope.

The best advice I got came from my neighbor, Steve Smith. He told me, "You have to look at this like any other engineering problem. You have to collect all the information and data you can, figure it out." He was right. I hadn't been dealing with the problem in the right way. I hadn't been to an eye doctor in two years. I'd lulled myself into believing that orthokeratology would be an easy fix, but that had been a way to avoid facing my fear head-on.

I would have known more about NASA's stance on ortho-keratology if I'd been up-front and asked, but I'd been too scared to bring up the subject of my eyes. I thought I could tiptoe around the problem when what I needed to do was tackle it: admit that I needed help and get help. I went back to JSC and went to see Smith Johnston. "What do I have to do?"

The first thing Smith told me was to take the lenses out. Not only were they not helping, but because I'd worn the same lenses for so long without getting them checked, they'd gotten old and scratched up and had damaged my eyeball, which was why Keith couldn't correct me to 20/20. So no contact lenses for six months—only glasses, to give my eyeballs a chance to heal.

I also started looking into vision training. Overfocus-ing of the eye muscles is one of the causes of nearsighted-ness. Vision training is a program of exercises that teaches you how to relax your eye muscles in order to improve your unaided acuity. It's not a miracle cure, but it can give you incremental improvements, which was what I needed. It just takes time. Smith told me to do that and keep get-ting checked by my eye doctor and send him the results. If I showed that I could pass, they could consider me for the next astronaut class.

I said, "Okay, if that's what I have to do, I'll do it."

•   •   •

Over the course of the next year, about a million things happened at once. Shortly after my flameout on the eye exam, we found out Carola was pregnant again. With two kids to support and the astronaut dream looking shaky, I had to think seriously about what I would do if it didn't pan out.

I liked the job at McDonnell Douglas, and it had been a great way to work closely with the astronaut office; but if I wasn't going to be an astronaut, I wasn't sure it was what I wanted to spend the rest of my life doing. I had started teaching some classes on the side at Rice University, which has a great engineering school and a long relationship with the space program, going back to the start: Rice's stadium is where President Kennedy gave his historic speech kicking off the Apollo program in 1962. Teaching brought in a little extra money, and in the back of my mind I always thought if the astronaut career didn't work out, academia might be my best fallback option. With the astronaut dream up in the air, I started sending out letters and résumés to different schools for full-time professorships. I got interviews with the University of Maine, Rensselaer Polytechnic Institute, the City College of New York, a few other places.

Then I got a call from Georgia Tech. Bill Rouse, a former student of Tom Sheridan's at MIT from before my time, was in the industrial engineering school there and he'd started a lab, the Center for Human-Machine Systems

Research. They were doing work with human factors and control systems and were looking to do more space-related work as well. I flew down and interviewed with them and they offered me a job.

Georgia Tech wanted me to start in January. I didn't want Carola to have to move while she was pregnant; she had her doctors and her support in Houston, and we wanted the baby to be born there. Also, my robot-arm display was set to be flown in space on STS-69 in June, and I wanted to be in Houston for that. So I asked if they'd wait until the fall semester. They agreed and let me push my start date to August.

For the next seven months, I had one major goal: fix my eyes. I found an optometrist who specialized in vision training, a woman named Desiree Hopping. First, she gave me a new pair of glasses with undercorrected lenses; they would take the strain off my focusing system and help my eyes to relax. Then she gave me some exercises. There was one where I had to stare at a bunch of marbles spaced out on a string at different intervals, shifting my focus to each one. I had to stare at different eye charts at different distances, the idea being that I would train my eye to relax and focus on an imaginary point beyond where the chart is, causing the letters on the chart to appear sharper. These exercises required deep, deep concentration. I had to do this dead stare for minutes at a stretch, no blinking. I looked like a serial killer giving you the evil eye. Some nights I'd go to bed and my eyes would be bloodshot from the strain of forcing them to relax, which sounds odd, but it's true.

I'd go to the office every day and work on my robot-arm display. Then I'd come home. We'd eat dinner, put Gabby to bed. Then I'd sit up at the kitchen table doing these vision exercises. My mother-in-law, who'd come down to help us while Carola was pregnant, would sit there with me, holding up these charts over and over again while I stared her down like a crazy person.

But it was working. I kept going back to Dr. Hopping every two weeks to get my eyes checked, and they were getting better, bit by bit. Then NASA threw me a curveball. After pushing the class of '94 back to '95, instead of waiting the normal two years to do the next selection, they were going to move ahead and do two classes back-to-back. They'd be taking applications that summer for a class to be picked in the spring of 1996. I'd thought I was going to have a whole year to get settled in Atlanta and slowly work on my eyes. Now the whole interview and selection process would happen right when I was moving. I resubmitted my application and prayed I'd be ready in time.

In the middle of all this, on July 5, 1995, our son, Daniel, was born. Having a girl was great, and having a boy rounded out the team. At that point our lives were up in the air and I was racked with doubt about the choices I was making. Daniel's arrival was just what I needed. It was a perfect blessing. Having those kids opened up a new dimension of love for me that I couldn't have dreamed existed. Whether I became an astronaut or not, nothing was more important than that.

Our real estate agent came by and told us she'd found someone to rent our house short-term. If I did get picked by NASA, we'd be able to come right back, which was nice to contemplate. The movers came and started packing us up, and I flew to Atlanta for a long weekend to race around and try to find us a place to live.

Apollo 13 came out that summer, and since I was by myself in Atlanta, I went to see it, but it was tough for me to watch. It was the best space movie since *The Right Stuff:* the astronauts and their families having parties in Houston, the whole NASA team pulling together to save these guys and bring them home . . . it was everything I was leaving behind, and I had no idea if I'd ever make it back. I sat there in the theater, loving the movie and being completely depressed by it. I flew back to Houston, collected Carola and the kids, and the first week of August we loaded up and headed east on I-10 with our whole lives packed into a moving truck. The house I'd found for us to rent in Atlanta turned out to be horrible. It looked okay to walk through, but the foundation was cracked and leaked whenever it rained. There were bugs. Nothing felt right.

Then, around the first of September, we had barely moved in when I got a call from Teresa Gomez in the Astronaut Selection Office asking me to fly back to Houston. They were looking at applications again, she said. Mine was in the good pile, and the flight surgeon said my eyes had improved enough that they were willing to let me come back and try again. There was one catch: I had to fly back in a month at my own expense and do the eye exam. If I passed, I'd be back in the running. If I failed, I was out of luck.

It turned out that my luck that fall was pretty good. I called my optometrist to let her know what was happening and she had some news for me. Apparently there were not many Landolt C machines in use, but there was one at the Emory Eye Center in Atlanta. Of all the cities in North America I could have moved to, I'd picked one with the machine that I needed. She suggested that maybe I call them up to see if I could go down there and use it. So I did. There were two very nice women who ran the Landolt C unit at Emory. I went down and talked to them and asked if they'd let me use their machine to practice. They said yes, and for the next few weeks, I went there every chance I got.

The first week of October, I flew back to Houston to sit with Keith Manuel and take the exam. He mapped my eyeball and it was healthy. He corrected me to 20/20, and that went fine. Then he had to test my unaided acuity on the Landolt C. In an eye exam, they want you to relax. They want to test your eyes at their natural resting state. My problem was that I had to work hard to relax. I had to strain my face to do this evil-eye gaze that forced my eyes to relax and focus properly. I was like a kid with a learning disability. I could pass the test; I just needed to work harder to do it.

And I did it. I passed. *I passed!*

Duane Ross called and told me I was back in the pool of eligible candidates. I could come back and interview the last week of October. I flew back to Atlanta, taught for two weeks, then flew right back to Houston. The whole month, I was going all out. I ran every day. I didn't eat an ounce of fat. I got my sleep. I wasn't taking any chances. Sunday morning, I went in for an intro briefing and took the written psych test. Starting Monday, I came back and did the ultrasounds, the camera up the rear end, everything I'd done the last time. On my way out, I stopped off to talk to Rainer Effenhauser about something. As I was leaving, he said, "We'll see you tomorrow for the eye exam."

I wasn't sure I'd heard him right. I said, "The eye exam? I already passed the eye exam."

He said, "Yeah, but that was three weeks ago. Something could have changed. It has to be done at the time of selection."

"But I *just* did it."

"No, no, no. That wasn't official. I'm sorry, Mike. This is what we have to do."

I couldn't believe it. It was like a punch to the gut. But it was what it was. You do what you have to do. The following afternoon, I went back to the optometrist's office to take the test again, only now it was a different setup. Bob Gibson was working off to the side, and two optometry students from the University of Houston were there as well. Bob and his colleague Keith Manuel were adjunct professors at the school, and students would often work in their office prepping patients and performing tests to get workplace experience.

A young woman administered my eye exam. She had to be about twenty-four years old. My whole life had been leading up to that moment. Everything I'd done, day in, day out, for over a decade, was going to be decided in the next half hour. She mapped my eyeball and put me on the Landolt C to test my unaided acuity. I sat down at the machine and started the evil eye to try to relax and focus. She said, "Sir, you need to relax your eyes." To her it looked like I was straining when in fact I was doing the opposite.

I said "I am relaxing" and kept right on with the evil eye. Because that was how I'd trained myself to do it.

She said it again. "Sir, relax your eyes. We won't get accurate data if you don't. Sir? I need you to relax. Sir?"

She would not stop. She kept raising her voice. Inside

my brain, I was losing it. I wanted to yell, *Young lady!
You have no idea what's going on here! You have no idea
how much time and heartbreak I've been through. This is
my whole life at stake. This is my little-kid-playing-in-my-
backyard-since-I-was-six-years-old dream on the line—and
you need to keep quiet!*

Of course I didn't say any of that. I nodded and said
"Okay" and did my best to ignore her, and finally she
started losing it. "Sir! Sir! Stop the test! Stop it! You cannot
do this!" Finally, Bob Gibson heard us and came over and
asked what was going on. "He's not relaxing his eyes," she
complained. "He's not complying with the test protocol."

Bob stopped the test and took me into his office. He
said, "Mike, what have you got the rest of the week? Why
don't you come by my office first thing Thursday morning and I'll administer your test myself." He could tell
I was frazzled, and he wanted to give me the chance to
take the test when I was fresh and my eyes were rested. I
scheduled a new appointment for Thursday and walked
out, feeling pretty upset about the whole thing.

Wednesday, I had my second selection committee interview. John Young was back at the head of the table
again, but there were several new faces as well. I did okay
and I could tell they liked me, but there were still a million reasons why I wouldn't get it, not the least of which
was the strong group of people to choose from. Also, I
could still fail the eye exam and none of it would matter.

Thursday morning came. I showed up at Bob Gibson's office. Walking in, I felt surprisingly calm, at peace. I'd done everything in my power to make myself eligible for the job, and at that point, there was nothing else left to do. Whether I passed the eye exam or not, I'd always be able to say that I gave it my best.

That said, I *really* wanted to pass.

Bob opened the door, asked me to come in, and said, "You know what, Mike? If you relax and think positive, I'm sure you'll do just fine." He sat me in the chair at the Landolt C machine and started to administer the test. I took a deep breath and went for it. When I finished, Bob showed me the results. He said, "Congratulations, Mike. You did it."

I sat there stunned. I couldn't believe it. I looked up at Bob with tears in my myopic-but-now-qualified eyes and said, "I passed? I can call my wife and tell her I passed?"

He nodded. I think he thought I was going to kiss him.

It had seemed so impossible, so crazy, that I would pull this off, but it worked. It *worked*. It was a miracle. I felt a relief even greater than the relief I felt after passing my qualifying exam. Because passing a qualifying exam falls in the realm of what's possible. Getting your eyes to see better than they normally see is close to impossible. It was proof that no obstacle in life is too great to overcome.

The next day, I went by Rainer Effenhauser's office for the results of my other medical tests. "Everything came back okay," he said. "Now leave. Get out of here before anybody has a chance to find anything wrong with you."

I went home to Atlanta. I concentrated on getting settled in at Georgia Tech. And I waited.

By January, I knew I'd made the second-to-last cut. The U.S. Office of Personnel Management started my background check. They call everybody: your family, your coworkers, your kindergarten teacher. No stone is left unturned.

During my interview week, I'd gotten to know Mark Kelly. Mark was a Navy pilot, and while we were waiting, he and the other Navy applicants had put together an email list to share information about the selection process. Mark was kind enough to put me on it. It was gossip, rumors, speculation. We were all trying to read the tea leaves, desperate for every scrap of information we could get.

April 19 rolled around. It was a Friday. An email popped up from a naval test-flight engineer. She had called Houston to check on something and she'd been told that the calls, good or bad, were going out Monday morning. The second I read the email, I shut down my computer, left my office, and went for a walk. I couldn't sit still. I must have walked the whole afternoon, my mind racing.

It was all I could do to get through that weekend in one piece.

I took Monday morning off from work. If it was bad news, I didn't want to be crying at my desk at the office. I wanted to be home and ready for the call when it came. So, naturally, I was on the toilet when the phone rang. Carola came to the door and said, "Mike, it's a guy from NASA."

I ran out and grabbed the phone. "Hello?"

"Mike? This is Dave Leestma from the Johnson Space Center. How are you doing today?"

I said, "Dave, I don't know. You tell me."

He laughed. "Well, I think you're going to be pretty good because we want you to become an astronaut, and we hope you're still interested in coming."

I said, "Yes! And in case you didn't hear me: *Yes! Yes! Yes! Yes!*"

I was screaming into the phone. Carola started screaming, too. Then Daniel started crying. I think Gabby was confused. When I hung up, I still didn't think it was real. I had this panic that maybe they'd called the wrong Mike Massimino. I picked up the phone and called them right back. Duane Ross answered.

"Yeah?"

"This is Mike Massimino again. I just wanted to double-check that you guys made the right call."

"Yeah. Don't worry. We did."

PART 3

THE REAL RIGHT STUFF

9

THERE'S MACH 1

Life changes fast when you become an astronaut. On the day NASA called and offered me the job, I was a university professor who spent his days in front of a chalkboard, lecturing a roomful of nineteen-year-old engineering students. Six months later, I was breaking the sound barrier in the back seat of a twin-engine supersonic jet.

After getting the call and wrapping up my final semester of classes, at the end of July, we packed up and drove home to our house in Texas, which was waiting for us right where we'd left it. We pulled into the old neighborhood and up our street to find our yard decorated with American flags and streamers and a bunch of welcome home signs, compliments of Steve Smith, our astronaut neighbor. One week later, on August 12, 1996, I reported to the Johnson Space Center for work as an astronaut candidate, or ASCAN. I drove up to the north entrance and flashed my badge, and the guard waved me through. It was the best feeling in the world.

The first week or so was mostly orientation. We were the largest astronaut class in the history of the space program, forty-four of us, thirty-five Americans and nine international astronauts. Every astronaut class gets a nickname. The original Mercury guys were the Original Seven, and the second group of nine were called, rather imaginatively, the New Nine. Once the shuttle era came, the names got more creative: the Maggots, the Hairballs, the Flying Escargot. The astronaut office takes up the entire sixth floor of Building 4 at the Johnson Space Center. The class before us had fifteen people, and space was already tight. Now they had to cram all of us in there. They called us the Sardines.

Once we arrived, NASA didn't waste any time getting us in the air. Shuttle astronauts fall into two groups, pilots and mission specialists. I was a mission specialist. All mission specialists are trained to fly as back seaters, co-pilots. The purpose of flying jets is spaceflight-readiness training. The different shuttle simulators are great, but they're not real. Flying a high-performance jet is as real as it gets. You're controlling a real airplane, working with a real pilot, communicating with a real air traffic controller, experiencing real nausea and real turbulence and real gut-dropping, nerve-racking, panic-inducing situations. It trains your mind and your body to feel, react to, and deal with how physically and mentally demanding spaceflight is going to be.

On the first day, they measured us for our flight suits. Military pilots wear green flight suits. Astronauts wear blue. The suit comes with the American flag on the left shoulder and the NASA logo on the right side of the chest. Most important, it's got your astronaut's wings. You can get white, silver, or gold. Most civilians get white. I ordered gold. They took a mold of my head for my helmet, traced an outline of my feet for my custom boots. Black or brown? Lace-ups or buckles? Everything is custom fit. They also give you leather/Nomex gloves and a watch, a Casio Illuminator on a black wristband with a small NASA insignia, informally called the NASA meatball, on its face. Then you top it off with cool sunglasses, Randolph aviators, standard military issue, with straight-back frames with no hook so you can slide them on and off while wearing your helmet—the same ones worn by the pilots in *The Right Stuff.* You can get your call sign printed on your helmet if you want, like you see in *Top Gun,* with guys like "Maverick" and "Goose" and "Ice Man." When I was a kid in school, a lot of kids didn't even know my real name was Mike. Everyone called me Mass. Then, at grad school and McDonnell Douglas, nobody called me that anymore. The name just went away. But once I became an astronaut, people started calling me Mass again. It fit. Soon it was the only thing people called me, and that became my nickname (or as pilots would say, my call sign), MASS, printed on my helmet.

To get us ready to fly, NASA shipped us out to the Naval Air Station in Pensacola, Florida, for water and land survival training. Then we were off to Vance Air Force Base for parachute training in Enid, Oklahoma, before heading back to Houston for three weeks of ground school, where we learned the aircraft systems, navigation, Federal Aviation Administration regulations, how to deal with inclement weather, flight plans—everything we needed to know to assist the front seater in flying the jet.

Flight operations for the Johnson Space Center were done out of Ellington Field, which is ten miles up the road toward downtown Houston. NASA has its own facilities there, a two-story office building attached to hangars for our planes: the WB-57 high-altitude research airplane, the shuttle training aircraft, the KC-135A zero-gravity airplane—the famous "Vomit Comet"—and our fleet of T-38s. Astronauts do spaceflight-readiness training in the T-38, a two-seat, twin-engine supersonic jet. It can go faster than the speed of sound and cruise at altitude around 700 miles per hour. Just imagine a Ferrari as a fighter jet. They're small and sleek, with razor-thin wings and a sharp needle nose, painted white with a blue racing stripe and NASA's logo on the tail. It's one of the coolest flying machines ever built.

My first T-38 flight was on October 30, 1996. It was a beautiful, clear autumn day.

I was going up with Frank Marlow, one of our flight

instructors. The back seater's main job is to handle the radio and the navigation. You can't land or take off, but you get to do nearly everything else: fly the route, approaches, aerobatics. The pilot takes you up and shows you how. He flies and then you fly. He demonstrates and you execute and that's how you learn to fly.

That day, Frank was taking me out to the practice area over the Gulf of Mexico south of Houston. The way it works is, you fly into that airspace and then radio air traffic control to let them know you're activating the practice area. Once you do that, no commercial traffic is allowed in, and it's yours to do whatever you want. It's like reserving a tennis court in the sky. NASA's practice area is called Warning Area 147-Charlie—about a thousand square miles that goes from 10,000 feet up to 26,000 feet. There you really have room to have fun.

Of course, you are also taught that, yeah, it's a lot of fun, but you're not there to only have fun. Flying is serious business. People die. Ted Freeman was the first fatality in the NASA Astronaut Corps when he was killed in a T-38 crash in 1964. Two Gemini astronauts, Elliot See and Charles Bassett, crashed in a T-38 in St. Louis in 1966. That same year, C. C. Williams died in a T-38 crash over the Everglades before he had the chance to fly in space, and Alan Bean replaced him on *Apollo 12*.

Frank and I were scheduled to go out at four thirty in the afternoon.

I climbed up the ladder and into the cockpit. Bob Mullen, the crew chief who had strapped the original Mercury Seven into their training jets, followed me up and helped me with my parachute straps and my mask and my helmet and everything else. He nodded, smiled, shook my hand, and said, "Have a good flight. See you in a bit." Then he climbed down and pulled back the ladder and I was on my own, about to go punch a hole in the sky. I did the radio calls to get runway clearance, and we taxied to line up on the runway, powered up the engines to make sure all was well, and then lit the afterburner. Frank released the brakes and we started accelerating, quickly. We were going over 150 miles an hour when Frank raised the nose and we shot up into the sky. I felt like I was riding a rocket ship.

Once you are in the practice area, there are a couple of things you have to do on your first flight, kind of like your initiation. The first thing is to go weightless. You fly up and push over and plummet straight down. Going weightless is an incredible experience. I was strapped in tight, but I could still feel myself floating up a bit. My pen was attached by a lanyard to my kneeboard and it floated up for a moment, slowly, like magic. Dust floated off the dashboard, too. The weightlessness lasted only for a few seconds, but it left me with an unmistakable feeling: I wanted more.

The second thing we did was break the sound barrier.

Frank flew us up to a high altitude, because you get more
speed flying down. Then you light the afterburner to get
as much thrust as you can. The plane started to shake and
I was pinned to my seat and watched the Mach meter
inching up: 0.95, 0.96, 0.97 . . . When we reached 1.0,
I said, "There's Mach 1," in my best Chuck Yeager impression, which was what I'd always dreamed of doing if
this day ever came. There's a boom in the sky as you pass
Mach 1, but I didn't hear it. You don't hear it, because
it's behind you. You're moving too fast—faster than the
speed of sound. And the view. *Wow.* Unlike in a commercial plane, under the T-38's clear canopy, I could see all
around me, a big blue sky spread out in every direction.
It gave me the sensation that I was zooming and swooping
through the air like an eagle.

I loved flying. I could not get enough of it. Back seaters
had to log a minimum of twenty-five training hours in the
T-38 every three months. I was always near the top of my
class in T-38 hours for backseaters. Some of my classmates
looked at flying like a chore. To me it was the ultimate
cool thing to do. My friend Alan Bean, who walked on the
moon on *Apollo 12,* told me that the key to a happy life
is to find something you love so much that you would do
it for free, and then find a way to make a living doing it.
That's exactly what I was able to do, and I am so grateful
I didn't give up on my dream. The best part was that you
could do it pretty much whenever you wanted. It wasn't

like getting to space, where you were sitting around, waiting to be assigned. You could hop in a jet and go. The instructors were test pilots out of Naval Air Station Patuxent River and Edwards Air Force Base. They loved having eager students because they loved to share the experience of flying, and they had the best stories: military exploits, launching off aircraft carriers, combat flights. Some of the older instructors had stories about showing legendary astronauts the ropes. These weren't the stories I'd read about in *Life* magazine. These were inside stories from the people who'd lived it, and I hung on every word. What amazed me was that they accepted me right away. I was a part of their military flying culture now. I belonged there. They were *Right Stuff* guys and we were flying together in *Right Stuff* planes doing *Right Stuff* stuff. They'd take me out and we'd do the craziest maneuvers: cloverleafs, aileron rolls, barrel rolls, Immelmann turns. It was unbelievable. What a job! What a life!

We'd usually stay out until Bingo time. On some military jets, the fuel indicator has a warning sound that goes *bing-o, bing-o,* to let you know you've hit a certain fuel level. So you'd say, "It's Bingo time," and head in. The coolest thing to do on landing was a touch-and-go. You'd make your approach and come in and radio tower, "Touch-and-go, request closed pattern." They'd come back with "Touch-and-go, closed pattern approved." You'd touch down, main wheels down, nose wheel down, then *BOOM!* you'd jam the throttle and *WHOOSH!* you'd take off again. Then you'd get your speed up and make a tight turn at high speed and go back into the traffic pattern. Then you'd go back and do it again. Then you'd go back and do it *again*. It was like riding the world's best roller coaster over and over without ever waiting in line.

I wanted to grow up to be Spider-Man—and I did.

10

SPACEWALKER

Other than flying in the T-38, one of my favorite parts of astronaut training was the enrichment lectures. Former astronauts and NASA legends would come visit and give talks about their experiences in the space program. Chris Kraft, NASA's first flight director, came in to speak with us. So did Gene Kranz, the flight director played by Ed Harris in *Apollo 13*. My favorite lecturer was Alan Bean, who flew on *Apollo 12* and is one of the twelve people who walked on the moon. After retiring from NASA, he became a painter. Alan's lecture was called "The Art of Space Exploration." He talked about the mistakes he'd made and how he learned to fix them. One lesson that took him a while to learn was that, at a place like NASA, you can have an effect only on certain things. You can't control who likes you. You can't control who gets assigned to flights or what NASA's budget is going to be next year.

If you get caught up worrying about things you can't control, you'll drive yourself crazy and waste valuable time. It's better to focus on the things right in front of you that you can control. Identify the places where you can have a positive impact. Concentrate there and let the rest take care of itself. The last thing Alan said to us was "What most people want in life is to do something great, and you have been given the opportunity to do something great. That doesn't happen often. Don't take it for granted. Don't be blasé about it. And don't blow it. A lot of times, believe it or not, people blow it."

Alan's lecture meant a great deal to me. I asked for a videotape of it and watched it again from time to time. It got me thinking about where I could have a positive impact on the space program. As an ASCAN, you have to learn everything there is to know about how the shuttle works. Flying a spaceship is not like driving a car. If you're driving a car and something goes wrong, the worst that happens is you pull over and wait for a tow. You can't do that in space. As an astronaut, you have to understand everything on that machine that could possibly go wrong—anything from a broken toilet to a leaking fuel tank. Even though you can count on help from Mission Control, it's going to be on you and six other people to fix the problem, whatever it is. So during your training you learn it all. You get a copy of the *Shuttle Crew Operations Manual,* our textbook. You study handouts and workbooks for each of the individual systems: This is how the fuel tanks work. This is how the pumps work. You participate in simulations—"sims" in NASAspeak—to test your knowledge of how everything works, how to respond when systems fail and how to work together and with mission control to solve problems. Sims are the backbone of your training as an astronaut. Because there's no margin for error in space, the solution to nearly every foreseeable problem has to be worked out before leaving the ground. You run through a scenario until you find a fault in your plan. Then you address that and you run through it again. Then you run through it again. Then you run through it again and again and again until every possible outcome has been accounted for.

With all that practice, if we encountered a new problem in space, we could figure out how to solve it even if a written procedure did not exist. I think that is a huge benefit of a STEM education, applicable to many fields: learning to solve problems as part of a team.

Once you've got the broad overview of the shuttle systems and operations down, that's when you're ready to graduate from ASCAN to astronaut. From there, pilots take their training in one direction, learning how to fly the shuttle, and the mission specialists begin to specialize in a variety of particular jobs: spacewalking, flying the robot arm, serving as flight engineers. After my ASCAN graduation, I still wasn't sure where I'd end up. I'd wanted to be an astronaut my whole adult life. I'd wanted it so badly, I'd never really cared what kind of tasks I would do in space; they all seemed great. The selection committee had chosen me not for any one particular skill but because they thought I had the general qualities of a good astronaut. I was still most all-around, I guess, same as in high school. For me, finding the place where I could contribute was my biggest challenge.

Then I went to another enrichment lecture and I found the purpose I was looking for.

In the spring of 1997, Story Musgrave came to talk to us about spacewalking, or extravehicular activity—EVA in NASAspeak. Story Musgrave served as the lead spacewalker on the first repair mission for the Hubble Space Telescope and was a very experienced spacewalker. He was an amazing guy, an MD with a master's in biophysics and another master's in literature that he went and got after becoming an astronaut, just because he was interested.

Developing the ability to put a human being outside a spaceship was one of those giant leaps that made human space exploration possible. Without it we couldn't service the Hubble Space Telescope, assemble space stations, or walk on the moon. There wasn't a great deal of EVA done in the early shuttle era. For the most part, those missions were deploying satellites, conducting Spacelab experiments, things that didn't require working outside the shuttle. All that was about to change. More Hubble servicing missions were on the books, and those would involve extensive EVA. International Space Station (ISS) assembly flights were about to get under way, too. Astronauts would be required to actually get out in space and put the ISS together, module by module, piece by piece. We called it the Wall of EVA, and it was coming up soon.

Most of the training for EVA takes place in the NBL, the Neutral Buoyancy Lab, which is a fancy name for an enormous swimming pool: 202 feet long, 102 feet wide, and 40 feet deep. In there astronauts worked with full-scale mock-ups of the space shuttle, the Hubble, and the space station. You get in the space suit and you're lowered into the water, attached to flotation devices that counterbalance the 200-pound suit you're wearing, making you neutrally buoyant and allowing you to move in an approximation of weightlessness. We practice underwater because although things sink in water (a rock or a boat anchor, for example), things can also float (like Styrofoam or a beach ball). In the NBL we use combinations of weights and floatation so that the force of gravity pulling us down is equaled by the buoyancy force pushing us up. The combinations are determined by scuba divers who assist us throughout a training run. When the combinations are where we want them, the forces cancel and we are neutrally buoyant, which means we float in the water column much like we would float in space. As part of the ASCAN

(Above left) Visiting relatives on a Sunday with my sister, Franny; Mom; and Dad. My brother, Joe, was the photographer.

(Above right) I loved Santa when I was four years old. I wanted a fire truck that year.

(Right) Franny, me, and Joe, all dressed up in front of our house.

(Left) With my copilot, Snoopy, July 1969. Backyard adventures in space.

(Right) My sixth-grade school photo with 1970s hairstyle.

(Above left) With my best friend, Mike Quarequio, before we take the field in the spring of 1973.

(Above right) I was a very skinny but enthusiastic basketball player in 1974.

(Center) One of my fondest memories: Dad and me on a Cub Scout camping trip in 1973.

(Below left) Summer baseball in high school with my lifelong friend Pat Adamo.

(Right) With Mom and Dad at my Columbia graduation. They are smiling because they thought my formal education was over. Little did they know . . .

(Above left) With one-year-old Gabby on my shoulders and space shuttle *Columbia* on top of a 747 at Ellington Field, 1994.

(Above right) With eight-month-old Daniel at Jekyll Island, Georgia, spring break 1996.

(Center) A very happy pose for my first official astronaut photograph.

(Left) All dressed up and about to be lowered into the water for a challenging day of spacewalk training at the Neutral Buoyancy Laboratory (NBL).

(Above) Flying at what we called "the speed of heat" in a NASA T-38 above the Gulf of Mexico.

(Right) With Dad, Mom, Carola, Gabby, and Daniel at astronaut class graduation—from astronaut candidates to official astronauts. April 1998.

(Below) The NASA astronaut class of 1996. The Sardines—thirty-five Americans and nine international astronauts, the largest (and best-looking) astronaut class ever. (Can you find me?)

(Top) Checking out the payload bay of space shuttle *Columbia* with Rick Linnehan (behind me). Our spacewalking instructor Dana Weigel is next to Rick and apparently falling asleep after a late night at the Cape.

(Center) The STS-109 taking a break from emergency training at the Kennedy Space Center. Space shuttle *Columbia* is in the background on the launchpad. Top row (left to right): John Grunsfeld, Scott Altman, Nancy Currie, and Jim Newman. Bottom row (left to right): Duane Carey, Rick Linnehan, and me.

(Below) With Mike "Bueno" Good (on the robot arm) training in NGL. Divers on the right are holding an IMAX camera and filming the documentary *IMAX: Hubble 3D*.

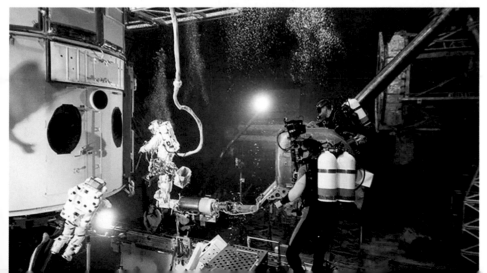

(Above) With Jim Newman (on left) exchanging an old for a new reaction wheel during our first spacewalk together.

(Left) The Hubble Space Telescope on the shuttle's robot arm as seen through an overhead window in the space shuttle. Beautiful planet Earth in the background.

(Below left) Trying to look relaxed and cool for my spacewalking hero photo, taken just minutes into my first spacewalk on STS-109. Notice Earth in my visor.

(Below right) Happy moment with Jim Newman after successfully completing our first spacewalk.

(Above) Rick Linnehan on the arm rotating a solar array, trying to not be distracted by the view of Earth in front of him. My turn came the next day during nightfall, so there was no worry about such distraction.

(Below left) Another boyhood dream fulfilled: throwing the ceremonial first pitch from the mound at Shea Stadium before a Mets versus Yankees subway series game, June 15, 2002.

(Below right) The crew of STS-107 in orbit just days before they did not make it back to Earth on board space shuttle *Columbia*.

(Above left) Space shuttle *Atlantis* lifts off on its mission to unlock the secrets of the universe. May 11, 2009, at 2:01 p.m. Eastern Daylight Time.

(Above right) Having mixed feelings as I prepare for entry and landing on my last day in space, May 24, 2009.

(Left) With my copilot, Snoopy, May 2009. Same Snoopy, but now with real adventures in space.

(Below) Going into a sunrise during the fourth and final spacewalk of my astronaut career.

training, every astronaut had to get certified in the basics of EVA by doing four runs in the pool. Before we could get in the water in the space suit, we had to pass a high-grade scuba certification. I had a civilian scuba license, but this was a more difficult test. The hardest thing for me was the unassisted ditch and don. You had to swim down to fifteen feet, take off (ditch) your mask and flippers, go back to the surface, tread water, then dive back down, put on (don) the gear, clear your mask, and get back to the surface with no water inside your mask. I couldn't do it. I'd get halfway through donning my gear and I'd start to panic and need a breath and I'd have to shoot back to the surface.

Fortunately, I was at NASA, and my weakness wasn't seen as an opportunity to weed me out. It was a chance for the team to get behind me. Charlie Hobaugh—nicknamed Scorch—was in my astronaut class. Scorch was *huge,* completely jacked, and a Marine pilot who served in Desert Storm and flew Harrier jets, the kind that can take off vertically and hover like a flying saucer. He was also one of the nicest guys on the planet. When he saw I was having trouble, he came by my office one morning, totally unsolicited, and said, "We're going to take care of this today." He found an astronaut with a backyard pool we could use and we drove over there. He sat in the pool with me and showed me what to do, showed me how to relax and get through it. All afternoon, he dove with me to the bottom of that pool, up and down and up and down. We started in the shallow end and gradually moved down to the deep end. He took me through it over and over until I got it. A week later, I passed the swim test.

When it was my turn to get in the pool wearing the EVA space suit, I was paired up with Charlie Camarda from Ozone Park, Queens. Charlie was the son of a butcher, a guy from the neighborhood, like me. He had a thick Italian mustache and a swoop of jet-black hair. Anytime you put me and Charlie together, we were like a couple of class clowns, like a two-man Three Stooges routine. We'd cut up and have fun. One of the things drilled into us during training was that spacewalkers had to stick close together, which led to me and Charlie on the test standing next to the pool, dancing in our full-body polypropylene underwear, and singing "Together, Wherever We Go," an old Ethel Merman show tune from *Gypsy*.

The instructors loved it. Outside the pool, Charlie and I were a hit. Inside, not so much. Your first training run in the pool is called the Introduction Suit Qualification, a few hours in the water to get used to the suit and demonstrate your ability to maneuver in it. They lowered me and Charlie in, and it was a wild underwater adventure. I tried to move around and felt like I was completely out of control. The suit is massive. I was stiff, clumsy. I felt like a Thanksgiving Day balloon, like the Michelin Man, the Pillsbury Doughboy. As I tried to translate down the side of the mock payload bay, inching my way along, I was thinking, *I'd better brush up on my robot-arm training, because this is not going to work.*

On a space walk, one astronaut is the free-floater and one astronaut is attached to the end of the robot arm. That way the arm operator can move them around to wherever they're needed. You attach yourself to the robot arm through a foot restraint by working your feet into toe loops and then spreading your heels to engage the locking mechanism. Your boot clicks into place. You can't spacewalk unless you can do it, and for the life of me, I couldn't do it. When you're wearing the space suit, you can't see your feet; and since you're in the water, if you lean forward to try to see your feet, you pivot around your waist and your feet go up behind you. You have to do it blind. I could maneuver into the toe loops, but I could never get my heels into the locks. I'd try and try and try until I reached the point where I was so frustrated and overworked that I couldn't get anything right. A few times the divers had to come over and put my feet in the restraints for me so that the training run could continue.

I reached out to my neighbor Steve Smith, who had spacewalked on both of the last two Hubble servicing missions. "Steve," I said, "I'm having a tough time."

Like Scorch, Steve had total confidence in me. He said, "Don't worry about it. We're gonna take care of this. You're gonna be great at it."

Steve volunteered to do a run with me. We went out to the NBL an hour and a half early. We went over everything outside the pool. Then we got in the water and he showed me how to use the foot restraints. The problem was that I wasn't getting my foot flat. I was getting my toes in the toe loops, but I wasn't pushing my heel far enough down. Steve worked on that with me, too. He'd tell me, "Try it quick one time. Flat and go! Flat and go! And you're in." I practiced it over and over again until I could finally do it on autopilot. Steve showed me how to use the tools, how to translate up and down the payload bay. I learned to stay calm and in control of my movements. By showing me what to do, Steve gave me the confidence to not panic in the pool. I got help from Steve, just like I'd gotten help from my Earth Science tutor in eighth grade. Some lessons learned in school go beyond the classroom.

Becoming proficient inside the space suit was a challenge—and that was a good thing. If there's one thing I learned about myself as an astronaut, it's that a challenge can force me to do my best. If I already know how to do something or if it comes easy, I don't always give it my best effort. But if you tell me something is impossible—if you tell me I can't pass my MIT qualifying exam or that I'm medically disqualified from becoming an astronaut—then from that point forward, for whatever reason, I'm incapable of giving up. I cannot let that problem go until I know I've done everything in my power to try to solve it.

11

SHACKLETON MODE

In the history of human exploration, I think there are basically two types of people. On the one hand, there are the scientists, people like Galileo Galilei. In seventeenth-century Italy, Galileo developed revolutionary telescopes, and with them he discovered the moons of Jupiter. He was the first person to identify the phases of Venus, proving Nicolaus Copernicus's theory of heliocentrism, that planets of our solar system revolve around the sun and not around the Earth. Scientists like Galileo work tirelessly in their laboratories, asking the big questions, and finding answers.

Then there are the adventurers, people like Ernest Shackleton. In 1914, Shackleton launched the third of his Antarctic voyages, the Imperial Trans-Antarctic Expedition—an attempt to cross the entire continent. His ship, the *Endurance,* was trapped and crushed in the

Antarctic ice. For over a year, first camping on the ice and then taking rowboats out across the open sea, he kept his men alive and led them safely to rescue on South Georgia Island, off the coast of Argentina. Men like Shackleton risked life and limb under punishing conditions to push the boundaries on the map, to expand our understanding of our world.

Some people dream of being Galileo. Other people dream of being Shackleton. An amazing thing about being an astronaut is that you get to be Galileo and Shackleton at the same time. You're tackling the big questions of human existence, and you're doing it in places where human life shouldn't even be possible. Down in the suburbs of Houston, driving around in our air-conditioned minivans, astronauts spend most of our time in Galileo mode, working on robot arms and other scientific endeavors. So, to learn how to survive in Shackleton mode, we have to leave the strip malls and the fast-food restaurants behind.

When people are put in extreme circumstances for a long period of time, or even just removed from their normal routine, they can get angry more quickly, teams can split apart, trust and communication can break down. Those outcomes are called "poor expedition behavior." With the launch of the International Space Station, long-duration spaceflights were going to be happening more and more frequently, and training astronauts to maintain good expedition behavior became a priority. I started hearing conversations about Shackleton around the astronaut office: How do we keep our crews together and functioning under impossible conditions the way he did?

As part of their contribution to the space station effort, the Canadian government offered to give astronauts cold-weather expedition training at its air force base in Cold Lake, a small town in northern Alberta that's home to a Royal Canadian Air Force base and weapons testing range. The Cold Lake expeditions started in 1999. Three of them were scheduled for the winter of 2000, one each in January, February, and March.

At the time, I was still waiting to get assigned to a shuttle flight.

I had no idea when I'd be assigned to fly in space. I was just working hard to improve in my EVA skills class, while keeping up with my day job in the robotics branch. Nancy Currie had taken over as head of the robotics branch the year before, and she showed me the value of having someone in my corner. She was a U.S. Army colonel with a PhD who'd recently completed her third flight, flying the robot arm on STS-88, the first space station assembly flight, in December 1998. At that point the robotics branch was focused on training astronauts to operate the new robot arm being developed for the space station. Nancy picked me to help her with that, and we ended up working together closely. She was smart and had a great sense of humor. She got to see me up close, to see how well I worked with the arm and how well I got along with the training team. She became one of my biggest boosters around the office.

Near the end of 1999, Nancy started talking me up to Charlie Precourt, the head of the astronaut office. Precourt was an Air Force test pilot, highly decorated, fluent in French and Russian, an incredibly accomplished and, to me, intimidating sort of guy. Charlie needed to assign a robot-arm operator for one of the flights, and Nancy told me Precourt came to her and asked, "Who do you recommend?"

She said, "Massimino."

He said, "Well, we need someone more experienced."

She said, "Massimino."

She told him I had the hands-on experience and was the right choice. Even with her recommendation, I got passed over for someone else. Precourt didn't think I was ready. Then Cold Lake happened.

I wasn't set to go on any of the expeditions that year, but as the March trip was coming up, somebody had to drop out. Precourt was going to be personally leading the group, and he announced at a staff meeting that they were short one person and needed a replacement. Nancy Currie put me up for it. Then she came to me after this meeting and said, "I kind of volunteered you to go to Cold Lake."

I said, "Are you out of your mind?!" I knew I'd probably have to go to Cold Lake at some point, but I wasn't jumping to volunteer. I'm still a kid from Long Island— natural outdoorsmen we're not.

She said, "No, it'll be good. You're going up there with Precourt."

I said, "Now I *know* you're out of your mind. You're gonna send me up to that frozen wasteland with the chief? With the boss? This is not going to go well."

Precourt was the guy who could make or break you when it came to getting assigned to a flight. I was petrified of screwing up in front of him. Nancy said, "No, no. Look, this will be good exposure for you, good training. Charlie's a great guy, and he needs to know you're a great guy. This is going to be a good way for you to get on his radar."

She was right. I didn't want her to be right, but she was. Then she said, "Oh, and you need to get packed. You leave in two days."

Cold Lake was given the name Cold Lake for a reason: There's a big lake, and it's really, really cold. One night when we were there, the temperature went down to minus 40 degrees Fahrenheit. But hey, it wasn't always that bad. Most nights it was a relatively balmy minus 20.

The expedition crew was Precourt and a bunch of relatively new astronauts who hadn't flown in space yet, including me; Lee Morin, a former naval flight surgeon;

Frank Caldeiro, who worked at the Kennedy Space Center as a propulsion system specialist before being selected to be an astronaut; and two of my astronaut buddies from MIT, Dan Tani and Greg Chamitoff. Greg had been selected by NASA two years after me, in 1998, and I wrote him a letter of recommendation—which I was thrilled to do, especially since he helped me pass my qualifying exam. Greg was also an Eagle Scout. He lived for this kind of outdoorsy survival adventure. I was glad to have him along.

We flew into Edmonton and then bused another two hundred miles north to the base. There we met our instructors, these four hard-core Canadian army special forces guys, the equivalent of our Green Berets. For them, going camping on a frozen lake in the dead of winter was like going to the beach. Sergeant Colin Norris was the team leader, a total tough guy, big mustache. We stayed in the barracks for a couple of days and they took us through some basic training: how to build a fire in the snow, set up tents, tie knots.

They also set us up with our gear. They gave us these old two-piece long johns, thick wool socks, bulky coats, and wool hats. We were issued Leatherman tools, navigation gear, and backpacks. The point was to expose you to the elements as completely as possible while giving us only the bare necessities needed to survive. We were in full Shackleton mode.

After a couple of days, it was time to head out into the field. Norris and his team helicoptered us out to the middle of nowhere.

We landed late morning in a clearing in a desolate, icy, snow-covered wilderness. It seemed endless. We unloaded our packs and our sled and our gear. Norris and his men timed us setting up our tent and trying to cook a meal for the first time. It was not easy; we were totally clueless and needed practice. Once we finally had everything set up, we watched the helicopter take off. As the helicopter flew away, leaving me and my five friends alone in the middle of the Canadian tundra, there was only one thought in my brain: *I'm cold*. I looked around and that's when it hit me. This is it, for ten days. I never realized how long ten days could be until I went to Cold Lake. For ten days I was never not cold.

We had to have the stove going inside the tent at all times; otherwise, it was too cold to do anything, which meant someone had to stay up on fire watch all night. We boiled snow for water to drink and heated up food in a pressure cooker. The tent didn't have a floor. We'd spread a foil sheet down under our sleeping bags and slept on top of the snow. It was dark most of the time, too. Late sunrise, early sunset. The Canadian army instructors would drop in on us once a day or so to check in and give us our objectives. We had only a few hours to get things done at 0 degrees before it fell back down to minus 20. We spent most of our time walking. As part of the exercise, every morning we'd break camp, trek to some new coordinates on the map, and set up camp again. Our gear would be loaded onto a sled, and we had to be our own sled dogs, hauling our gear across the frozen tundra. We had a GPS device, but it wouldn't always work, because the batteries would get too cold and stop working. I could use it for a couple of minutes, and then I had to hold it against my body to warm it up again. The point of the exercise was to induce stress. Over the course of a normal expedition, it might take months for the stress to get to people. But we had only a couple of weeks in Cold Lake, so they had to accelerate the process.

This expedition was *rough*. Maybe we weren't stranded at the South Pole, but it was no joke. All kinds of things went wrong. One night the tent caved in on us and we had to tie it to a tree. One afternoon Lee Morin and I went out and got lost. We were so lost, we didn't even know we were lost; that's how lost we were. At one point we ended up following our own tracks, thinking they were taking us back to camp, but actually we were taking ourselves in a circle. We barely made it back to the others before dark.

Halfway through, Frank Caldeiro hurt his knee and had to be helicoptered out. I got water in my boot and ended up with frostbite that didn't completely go away until months after the expedition. Cold Lake was so cold, I couldn't have any skin exposed outside the tent. Ever. I forgot that one day when I was trying to tie a knot. I got frustrated with having big, clumsy gloves on. I pulled the gloves off and my skin was exposed for barely a second and it was like someone had taken an ice pick and jammed it through the middle of my palm, just a terrible, searing pain. At that point, I thought, *This is ridiculous. This stinks. I'm cold, I'm tired, I'm miserable. I want to go home and watch television and use a real toilet. Why are we even here? Why am I even doing this?* That was my own poor expedition behavior. Which meant the exercise was a total success. It pushed me to the point of having those feelings so I'd know how to recognize and cope with them.

One of the things our Canadian taskmasters would do was show up out of nowhere and give us spontaneous tasks. One time we had to move camp in the middle of the night: break everything down, load it, haul it, and set up somewhere else, in pitch-blackness at 20 below. They would also periodically drop food and supplies at random points and send us off to find it and bring it back to camp. Sergeant Norris came up to me with a map at dinnertime one night. He said, "Massimino, at three a.m., you and a team member are going to go to these coordinates across this lake and find a box of food and retrieve it."

I said, "I have to walk across that lake in the middle of the night?"

"Yeah."

"Are you sure it's frozen? I don't wanna fall in."

He looked at me. "You do realize that we're standing on a lake right now, right?" He stamped his foot. *Thump! Thump! Thump!* "Don't worry. You'll be fine."

Then I asked, "But what will it look like out on the lake in the middle of the night? What will we be able to see?" Sergeant Norris answered, "Close your eyes. . . . That's what you'll see. Nothing."

I asked Chamitoff, the Eagle Scout, to go with me. Greg was having a grand time out in the wilderness; at one point he'd rigged up a shower for himself to bathe in the freezing cold. To me, that was crazy, but I also knew Greg was the guy I wanted with me so I wouldn't lose a leg to frostbite or get eaten by a bear.

In the middle of the night, we woke up and set off. We were halfway across the lake when we stopped and looked up. It was a perfectly clear night and the air was crisp and the stars were magnificent. There was no sound other than our breathing. Everything was perfectly still for miles around.

It hit me at that moment: I was having an extraordinary experience. I was out at the edge of civilization. Yeah, I was cold and, yeah, it was hard, but I was doing something amazing in spite of myself. I was learning new things about myself. I was being given the chance to step outside of my everyday life and look at the world in a completely different way. The world that had seemed so small growing up in Franklin Square was now vast and wide-open and filled with incredible, beautiful things. I turned to Greg and said, "Hey, remember how a few years ago we were a couple of kids in a dorm room, dreaming about becoming astronauts? And now here we are."

"Yeah," he said. That was the last either of us spoke. We just stood there, two buddies gazing out at the universe from the top of the world.

The whole trip changed for me halfway across that lake. The conditions hadn't changed, but my mind-set had, and that's what expedition training is for. I started to enjoy what I was doing. I started to appreciate the opportunities to learn new things, and the days flew by.

Survival training was not the point of the trip. We had food and water; they gave it to us. The goal was expedition training, learning how to deal with harsh, extreme circumstances. Shackleton's Antarctic expedition was unsuccessful in its original exploration goals. His ship was destroyed. He never reached the South Pole. Yet today he's revered because he kept his men together through such a catastrophic situation. He kept them focused on what needed to be done. He kept their minds active. He kept morale up. Shackleton was a great leader, and in any remote, difficult situation, leadership is key.

In Cold Lake, during our different tasks and exercises, we took turns leading the group. Before going up there, I was never comfortable in leadership roles. Now, for two out of the ten days of our expedition, I had to be the guy in charge—which was especially awkward because I was far and away the least experienced guy out there. Chamitoff was the Eagle Scout. Morin was older than me and a highly decorated officer who'd served in the Gulf War. Precourt was my boss. But I had to give the orders. I wasn't comfortable with it, so I handled it the way I try to handle most things: with humor. I kept trying to get everyone to laugh and stay loose, hoping to keep morale high to make up for the fact that I was in way over my head.

At the end of each day the Canadian instructors would grade us on how we did. What Sergeant Norris told me was something I never would have thought of: Humor is a great leadership tool. Most leaders, even if they're naturally funny, they'll get serious in front of the group and try to motivate people by cracking the whip. But if you can keep people laughing while they're freezing their butts off, that's good, too. My team completed its tasks and ended the day ready to go back out and do it again, which meant I'd done a good job. Precourt even took me aside and said he thought I'd done well. Nancy Currie was right. I was nervous about going out with the head of the office, worried that he'd see me making mistakes. And he did see me make mistakes, but he also saw me work hard and get better. He saw what my strengths were.

• • •

About a month after my Canada trip, Nancy Currie and I went to Japan to work with a team of engineers with the Japan Aerospace Exploration Agency (JAXA) at their facility in Tsukuba Science City, a couple hours outside of Tokyo. The Japanese were working on a different robot arm, one to help conduct experiments outside the station and bring them into an air lock. It was incredible to go to a place like Japan and be there as an astronaut and not as a tourist. For American astronauts to visit the Japanese space agency was a big deal. We were treated like big shots, VIPs. They wanted to hang out with us. Neil Armstrong and John Glenn still cast a long shadow. When it came to the work on the robot arm, my opinion was very, very important to these engineers. Every point I made or problem I pointed out, they were hanging on every word. It was another reminder of how much power and responsibility comes with the position.

The experience was similar to when I first became an astronaut and people started treating me with deference and respect because of my job title. Back then, I didn't feel like I'd earned it. This time it was different. This time I *felt* like an astronaut. I had been working and training for almost four years. My knowledge of the space program had increased a hundredfold. I was part of a team of extraordinary people. I'd overcome challenges and obstacles and proven to myself that I was capable of doing things I never would have thought I could do. It's a funny thing.

In the beginning, I felt like an impostor telling people I was an astronaut because I hadn't even been to space. Then I eventually realized that I was thinking about it all wrong. Going to space doesn't make you an astronaut. Being an astronaut means you're ready to go to space.

PART 4

THE DOOR TO SPACE

12

SEEING BEYOND THE STARS

The Hubble Space Telescope ranks right up there with the Pyramids and the Great Wall of China as one of the great engineering triumphs in human history. It's named for Edwin P. Hubble, the astronomer who discovered that galaxies like ours exist outside the Milky Way and first established that the universe is expanding—the scientific breakthrough that led to the big bang theory. Scientists were theorizing about the advantages of putting a telescope in space almost as soon as people started building rockets. A space-based telescope would be able to observe light undistorted by the turbulence in Earth's atmosphere. It would also be able to observe ultraviolet and infrared light, both of which get absorbed by Earth's atmosphere. A space-based telescope would be able to see things and learn things beyond what any human had ever dreamed.

The Hubble does all of that and more. It takes thermal

images of faraway planets, helping determine which ones might be capable of supporting carbon-based life. It measures the distance between stars with incredible accuracy. It's shown us how fast the universe is expanding and exactly how old it is (13.8 billion years, in case you were wondering). Hubble discovered Pluto's four new moons. It helped us learn about how stars are born and how black holes are formed. Much of what the telescope has discovered are answers to questions we didn't even know how to ask. The Hubble is, without question, the single most important tool humankind has ever had for understanding the universe and our place in it.

When the Hubble launched, it was the biggest story in space exploration since the launch of the shuttle itself. It had been in development since the early 1970s and was supposed to be deployed in 1983; technical delays kept pushing it back. In December 1985, I was still working at IBM, rushing through Penn Station to catch my train, when I glanced at a newsstand, and the cover of *Life* magazine caught my eye. It showed a spacewalking astronaut pulling open a tear in the fabric of space to reveal a distant yellow-orange nebula. The headline read: SEEING BEYOND THE STARS: A PREVIEW OF AMERICA'S BIGGEST YEAR IN SPACE. I grabbed a copy and read it right away on the train.

Because of the *Challenger* accident, 1986 turned out to be a big year in space for all the wrong reasons. The shuttle was grounded, and the telescope's deployment was pushed back again, to 1990. By the time it finally launched, what was supposed to be a $575 million project had ballooned into a nearly $1.8 billion project—and only after it launched did we discover it didn't work. The telescope's eight-foot-diameter mirror was defective, having been manufactured incorrectly. At its perimeter, it was too flat by approximately 2.2 micrometers—less than the width of a human hair—but it was enough that the telescope was bending the light incorrectly and wasn't able to focus.

Fortunately, we had the opportunity to fix it. Sophisticated, high-performance machines are temperamental. They need tender loving care to keep working correctly, and the Hubble is no different. That's why it was built to be serviced by astronauts. When it was launched, NASA had originally budgeted for four servicing missions that would go up and make repairs and upgrade the telescope's equipment as newer technology became available. After the problems with the mirror were discovered, the first of those servicing missions became a rescue mission.

The mirror itself couldn't be replaced. At eight feet in diameter, it's too big, and it isn't modular like some of the other components of the telescope. But even though the mirror had been manufactured incorrectly, it was incorrect with such precision that engineers knew *exactly* how much it needed to be adjusted, and they were able to fit it with corrective lenses: They gave it glasses, essentially.

The first Hubble servicing mission, STS-61, was launched in 1993. That crew installed the COSTAR, or Corrective Optics Space Telescope Axial Replacement, a device that put coin-size mirrors into the light path to bring the telescope's imagery into perfect focus. STS-61 was probably, up to that point, the most important shuttle flight in the history of the program.

The second servicing mission flew in February 1997. As intended, that mission was mostly routine maintenance, a 30-million-mile checkup. They replaced some worn-out equipment and installed two major new instruments: the Space Telescope Imaging Spectrograph (STIS) and the Near Infrared Camera and Multi-Object Spectrometer (NICMOS). The third mission was originally supposed to be routine maintenance and upgrades as well, the 60-million-mile checkup. Then, in 1998, Hubble's gyroscopes started to fail, one after another, much sooner than expected. Fine, hairlike electrical wires suspended in the fluid inside the gyros were corroding, something the engineers never anticipated. Of the six gyros on board, at least three needed to be working in order for the telescope to perform its functions. As they continued to fail, engineers put the Hubble into an emergency low-power mode, like putting a laptop to sleep. It was alive and it wasn't falling out of the sky, but it wasn't taking any pictures or doing any science.

The third servicing mission became an emergency

flight to replace all six gyroscopes. Some of the scheduled upgrades had to be postponed while the telescope was rescued—again. NASA needed to add an extra servicing mission. So Servicing Mission 3 was split into two parts: Servicing Mission 3A to rescue Hubble, and Servicing Mission 3B to perform the upgrades originally scheduled for SM3. Servicing Mission 3A launched right before Christmas in 1999. That crew got Hubble working again. Now NASA had to put together Servicing Mission 3B to handle the remaining repairs that 3A didn't complete, which meant that a whole new flight and a whole new crew had to be assembled from the ground up on short notice.

From the telescope's deployment through all three servicing missions, no rookie had ever spacewalked on Hubble. The work was incredibly complex and the stakes were considered too high. If something went wrong on a station assembly flight, we always had the opportunity to go back and fix it or have the onboard space station crew take care of it later. With Hubble, there was no margin for error. Now, though, with so much EVA needed for the station, it was decided that the fourth spacewalking position on the team might go to someone new. The chance to spacewalk on Hubble was probably the most coveted assignment in the entire astronaut office. I wanted it the same as everyone, but I didn't imagine I'd be in the running for it.

When I came back from Japan, I was transferred from robotics to the EVA branch, which was being led by John Grunsfeld, who'd just come back from spacewalking on Hubble Servicing Mission 3A. Grunsfeld is the smartest guy in the room, even at a place like NASA, where everybody's already smart to begin with. MIT undergrad, University of Chicago PhD. He's an astronomer, and he loves the Hubble Space Telescope as much as anyone has ever loved anything. He's also mechanically inclined, which made him a perfect fit for the Hubble servicing missions. Even with all the astronauts who'd worked on Hubble in the past, Grunsfeld was well known as the go-to expert on the telescope around the office. Shortly after I was transferred, Grunsfeld came up to my office one day and told me that he and Precourt wanted me to work on the development runs for Servicing Mission 3B.

Development runs are different from training runs. Training runs train the astronaut. Development runs are more for the engineers. Whenever they devise a new tool or a new method for tackling an issue—they've built a new ammonia tank, for example, or they need to repair and replace a cooling system—they need to try it out, test the device, test their hypothesis and their hardware. The astronaut's job is to get in the water and help the engineers work out the new procedures and designs. This works, this doesn't. This is good, this is bad.

I knew it was a huge opportunity, but I had no idea

how huge until the day we started. The briefings for the development runs were being held in the planning area outside the pool at the Neutral Buoyancy Laboratory (NBL). Every other time I'd been called in for a development run, we had maybe a couple of mid-level engineers briefing us on whatever project they were doing. But the moment I set foot in that first Hubble development run, I knew I wasn't in Kansas anymore. It wasn't like any briefing or any meeting or any sim (simulation) I had ever been to at NASA. They had the full-size mock-up of the telescope and different instruments and tools and machines laid out. There had to be at least thirty, forty people there. The veteran astronauts who'd flown on the first three servicing missions—several of them were on hand. This was the A-team.

There are days when opportunity knocks, days that define a turning point in your life. There is everything before that day and everything after it, which is permanently different. This was one of those days.

We did development runs through April and May. During one of the briefings when we took a break, I was standing under the NBL mock-up of the telescope, looking up at it. Grunsfeld was standing next to me. I said, "John, this mission is really important. I hope my run goes well."

He said, "I hope it goes well for you, too."

I said, "What do you mean?"

"You must realize you're on the bubble."

"What does that mean?"

"You're on the bubble of getting assigned. You're in the mix now. If these development runs go well, this is going to help."

I was speechless. I'd been hoping to get assigned to a spaceflight, any spaceflight. But Hubble? That was too much to hope for. As crazy as the idea seemed in my head, though, Grunsfeld didn't seem to think it was crazy at all.

What I think Grunsfeld and Precourt both recognized was my determination. Every obstacle that was put in my way, every challenge that I faced, I doubled down and worked harder and figured it out and got past it. And that's the kind of person you need on a mission where failure is not an option.

From the moment Grunsfeld told me I was in the mix, that telescope became my world. For the next two months, I did everything I could to learn everything there was to know. I watched tapes of the previous servicing missions. I sought out the guys who'd spacewalked on Hubble before and picked their brains for information. I went and talked to the engineers from the Goddard Space Flight Center who'd been working on the telescope for the past twenty years, absorbing all of their knowledge and experience. We'd get a briefing on Friday for a development run happening Monday, and I would go in on Saturday to walk through the steps on the mock-up to make sure

I knew everything and was completely prepared before going in the water. Even if it wasn't my turn to go in the water, I cleared my schedule and went and observed.

The guy I leaned on the most was Steve Smith. In addition to helping me in the pool when I was learning to spacewalk, Steve was a neighbor and great friend and had been to Hubble twice. I was constantly asking him questions, picking his brain.

Steve was also Charlie Precourt's deputy, so he knew a few days before everyone else who was going to get assigned to flights. That August, on the Friday before my birthday, Precourt let Steve know that I was going to get assigned to the next Hubble servicing mission—the first rookie ever to spacewalk on Hubble. Normally, you find out you've been assigned when Precourt calls you personally, but Steve asked if he could be the one to tell me. Precourt said, "You can tell him, but you can't tell him until Monday."

"But it's his birthday on Saturday," Steve said. "I can't tell him on his birthday?"

"No."

The whole weekend went by. We spent Saturday together, taking our kids to Home Depot to get wood for school projects, and Steve said nothing. Then, on Monday morning, I was getting ready for work and Carola came in and said, "Steve's here." I thought, *What is Steve doing here at seven thirty in the morning?* I went to the front door to meet him. He handed me an illustrated children's book about the Hubble Space Telescope. I said, "What the heck is this for?"

"I think you better read up on this, buddy," he said, "because you're going to Hubble."

13

READY TO GO

Joining a shuttle crew takes you into an entirely different phase of being an astronaut. If NASA is like a team, a shuttle crew is like a family. My new family was the crew of STS-109, Hubble Servicing Mission 3B. We would be flying on space shuttle *Columbia,* scheduled to launch in exactly eighteen months, in February 2002. Because this mission had so much EVA, the spacewalkers were assigned several months before the rest of the flight crew to give us extra time to prepare. In addition to me, the others were John Grunsfeld, Jim Newman, and Rick Linnehan.

Grunsfeld would lead the space walks on days one, three, and five. He had the most experience, having spacewalked on Hubble before. Newman would lead the space walks on days two and four. Linnehan had flown but never spacewalked, and I was the pure rookie. He was paired with Grunsfeld for three space walks. I was teamed with Newman for the other two.

Jim Newman and I knew each other from working together on computers and robotics; he was the astronaut
responsible for flying and testing my robot-arm display
when I was at Georgia Tech. We'd worked together for
almost ten years, and now we were going to be spacewalking together. His nickname was Pluto, because he
was in a whole different orbit.

Rick Linnehan was someone I didn't know that well before being assigned. Rick had an interesting background
for an astronaut: He was a large-animal veterinarian. He
started out doing research at Johns Hopkins University
and the Baltimore Zoo before going on to do marine mam-
mal research with the U.S. Navy. Very funny, loved dancing to Johnny Cash and doing old Three Stooges routines
while floating in space.

A few months later the rest of the crew was announced.
Scott Altman—"Scooter"—became our commander. He
and I were already old pals from five years of being neighbors and reenacting scenes from *Top Gun* on T-38 flights.
Nancy Currie was named our flight engineer and robot-
arm operator. She was and continued to be an ally and
advocate for me. She was a real veteran, too. Both she and
Newman had flown on the first station assembly flight, so
she brought some good experience in dealing with a high-
profile, high-pressure situation, which we were going to
need.

Duane Carey—"Digger"—became our pilot. Digger

was the other rookie on the flight besides me. He was your classic Edwards Air Force Base test pilot, loved riding motorcycles—a real *Right Stuff* kind of guy. He looked the part, too, with the crew cut and everything. We bonded quickly as the only rookies and are still close friends today.

After STS-109 was over, Charlie Precourt told me why he'd chosen me. I was a good spacewalker, but so were a lot of people. The thing that set me apart, to him, was my personality. No matter how stressful the situation, I try to keep things light and fun, like I'd done up in Cold Lake, like I'd done going back to elementary school. This was going to be a difficult mission in a high-pressure situation. There were all these very different, very strong personalities sitting around the family dinner table, and having a fun little brother sitting down at the end broke the tension and balanced everything out. I didn't know that was my job at the time, but in hindsight it made perfect sense.

Once the team was assembled, we threw ourselves into the mission. We had a full slate of tasks ahead of us.

There's an old NASA saying that I learned: "No matter how bad things appear, remember, *you* can always make them worse." It's true. Once a problem comes up, if you panic or act too fast, you will only exacerbate it. As a rookie, I was worried that I'd be the guy making things worse. I wanted to do my best and give the team a chance to recover if a problem did arise, not make it worse.

Fortunately, if there's one thing NASA knows how to do, it's condition people to deal with fear. No training experience on Earth can ever re-create exactly how it feels to be in space. So what NASA does is break the experiences of spaceflight and spacewalking down to their constituent parts. It's a lot like how studying for a test or practicing a sport or performing in front of an audience can help you feel less frightened. If you listen to your teachers and coaches and work hard, it's not as bad as you anticipated. Preparation builds confidence. It's no different in space.

For spacewalking, we have the pool. That's the major training tool because that's where the experience is as close as it will be in orbit. Water, however, creates drag. If you lose control of an object in the pool, it will eventually slow down and stop; if you lose control of an object in space, it will keep going and going and going and going.

Another thing that's different is the visual. The mock-up is not the same as the actual telescope, because it's made for the pool. The actual equipment is so sensitive it can't be put in the water, so it has to be a bit different. To work with the real equipment, we'd go to the Goddard Space Flight Center in Maryland. There they have a gigantic clean room, a room with a positive airflow so that no dust can ever form. Just to get in, I'd have to take an air shower to blow off the dirt and loose skin on my clothes. Then I'd have to put on a gown, a hood, a mask, gloves, and booties over my shoes. Then I'd walk through an air lock into a huge, warehouse-size room with guys in bunny suits walking around with clipboards and cranes moving equipment overhead. It felt like a scene out of a James Bond movie.

In the clean room, there was a high-fidelity, life-size mock-up of the telescope, a perfect replica: the exact same instruments, how they feel, what they look like. It's especially accurate on the inside, down to the intricate switches and the latches and the connector pins. The tools we used there were exactly the same as the tools we would be using in space. In the clean room, we'd work with this replica, mating the new solar array to the telescope, aligning and installing the new science instruments. We'd memorize what everything looked like, how the pins and connectors lined up, how they fit together. We'd practice over and over and over again until we could do it blind-folded.

The downside at Goddard is that we were in Earth's gravity. The EVA suit weighs over 200 pounds. The solar array weighs 640 pounds. We couldn't actually move any of this equipment around the way we would need to in space. To practice mass handling, we went to a virtual-reality lab. There, we had a machine we called Charlotte because it looked like an enormous spider in a web. It was a box with different handrails and wires coming off it. I'd put on the virtual-reality helmet and move the handrails around; they were programmed to behave as if I were manipulating a 640-pound king-size mattress in the vacuum of space, where the tiniest misstep could send the thing wobbling out of control.

We would be replacing the telescope's solar arrays with newer, more efficient ones. In the virtual-reality lab I would slowly, *slowly,* rotate the array: Right hand moves an inch. Left hand moves an inch. Right hand moves an inch. Left hand moves an inch. Then I'd rotate it on the air-bearing floor: Right hand moves an inch. Left hand moves an inch. Right hand moves an inch. Left hand moves an inch. I'd rotate it in the pool: Right hand moves an inch. Left hand moves an inch. Right hand moves an inch. Left hand moves an inch. For months and months and months.

Not one of these training exercises is exactly the real thing by itself. Each one mimics a certain aspect of being in space. I'd work with the real equipment in the clean room at Goddard and get a sense of what it was going to look like. Then I'd file that memory away. I'd play out the scenario in virtual reality and get a sense of how the mass handling was going to feel. Then I'd file that memory away. I'd do it again on the air-bearing floor and file that memory away. Then, piece by piece, I was synthesizing that information into a mental model of what the experience was going to be like once I was in space.

With each passing day the size and the scope of the mission seemed to grow larger.

There were times I felt completely overwhelmed. Going to space had been my dream for so long, sometimes I felt like it might *still* be a dream, like I was going to wake up and realize I was just an average Joe and had imagined the whole thing.

It's called impostor syndrome, the fear that people are going to figure out that you don't belong, that you don't know what you're doing. You're afraid that one day somebody's going to tap you on the shoulder and say, "Mike Massimino? Yeah, there's been a mistake. We meant to pick the other guy." It's natural to have those thoughts, but too often I'd let them get in my way. Because I was the rookie and the only crew member still in his thirties, I fell into the role of being everybody's kid brother, asking questions and letting others take the lead and show me what to do. I wanted to be humble, never arrogant, which is a trait astronauts despise. But the downside of that is that I'd slipped into a subordinate role. But I would need to step up and be a leader when the time came.

Even being the junior spacewalker, I still had to be in charge of my own tasks. I had to be confident and comfortable making decisions on the fly, telling my crewmates what I needed them to do when I needed them to do it. That kind of leadership didn't come easily for me. Sometimes during sims, I would get caught up in something and I'd be so worried about making a mistake or a bad

decision that I'd end up making a mistake or a bad decision. I was so concerned about being a rookie and accidentally breaking something that I tried to make up for
it by studying and asking questions constantly. At times
I went overboard in that regard. Asking too many questions betrayed my lack of confidence and gave some people the impression that I wasn't prepared and didn't know
what I was doing. John Grunsfeld tried to help. During
one of my evaluations, he said, "Mass, I believe in you,
and I believe that you can do this. Your problem is that
you don't believe in yourself."

One evening right before launch, Steve Smith came
over to my house to talk. I'm sure he could tell what I
was feeling. He said, "Mass, I want you to remember two
things. One: Know that you're prepared. You may not feel
like you're prepared, but they wouldn't let you go if you
weren't. And two: Space is an open-book exam. You're not
alone up there. This is a team, and you can always get help
if you need it."

That night was a real turning point for me. John and
Steve were both right. I had to stop thinking of myself as a
rookie. I was not a rookie in the eyes of Hubble engineers
and astronomers and management and instructors—I
was one of the guys who was going to fix the Hubble.
I couldn't leave my responsibilities to my crewmates. I
was fully capable and, more important, during eighteen
months of training, I had demonstrated that I was fully

capable. Everyone from the NASA administrator to our janitorial support in the NBL had confidence in me; now, for the sake of the team, I needed to have the same confidence in myself. Accepting that and knowing that was one of the hardest parts of preparing for the mission.

14

WEIGHTLESS

The first thing I did in orbit was my Tom Hanks routine from *Apollo 13,* taking off my helmet and floating it in front of me. Then I took my gloves off one at a time and floated those in front of me as well. I looked away to do something and when I looked back up, one of the gloves was gone; it had floated off. That was rookie space lesson number one: Hold on to things. They get away from you.

I started unbuckling myself from my seat. Rick was already out and heading up to the window to take a picture of the external tank, which had just separated, before it dropped away from us and burned up on reentry; this was to see if there was any external damage or loss of insulation foam that needed to be documented. I was right behind him. I had to get up to the window and take a look outside. John Glenn's view of Earth in *The Right Stuff* was the thing that had rekindled my space dream, and now, twenty years later, it was my turn to see it for myself.

We were over the Indian Ocean, which was a beautiful shade of blue with puffy white clouds sprinkled across it. I felt like I was in one of those dreams where you're magically floating above everyone else. I could see the ripples in the ocean, the horizon with the blue atmosphere in a thin, hazy line. It was like all the pictures I'd seen, only a thousand times better. I lingered for a moment, staring out. Then it was time to go to work.

The shuttle's crew compartment is small, only 2,325 cubic feet for seven people to live and work in for nearly two weeks. Up on the flight deck is where you get the amazing views, with six forward-facing windows for the pilots to fly the ship, plus two windows in the roof and two in the aft bulkhead looking out at the payload bay. In the floor of the flight deck is an opening leading down to the mid-deck, virtually every inch of its walls taken up by storage lockers and the gear needed to live and eat and sleep in space. On the aft wall of the mid-deck is the air lock leading out to the payload bay. The air lock is a cylinder with a round, forty-inch hatch leading to a space that's about five feet in diameter and seven feet long, just enough room for two astronauts in EVA suits to wait to go out on a space walk.

Scooter and Digger were up above us on the flight deck, checking out the systems, doing engine burns to put us on the right trajectory to rendezvous with Hubble. The rest of us were busy on the mid-deck going about the tasks necessary to convert the shuttle from a rocket ship to a spaceship: setting up the toilet, the galley, the exercise bike. That takes a couple of hours, in large part because adjusting to being weightless takes time.

From the minute I started moving around, I felt like a bull in a china shop. In the space station, astronauts can barrel themselves down the tube and get up some speed and fly like Superman or Supergirl. You can't do that on the shuttle. You can spin around, leap from the floor to the ceiling, but that's about it. On the first day, even doing that is difficult. Your sense of motion is all messed up. You feel crazy out of control at first, or at least I did. I'm naturally clumsy, plus I'm big, and I didn't know my own strength. I was banging into everything, knocking into people. One time my finger accidentally banged into a control panel wall and flipped a switch. There's switches and instruments all over the shuttle—over two thousand different displays and controls on the flight deck alone— and you don't want to go around randomly turning things on and off. That's bad. So you move slowly, awkwardly, trying to develop some sense of control. The whole process is like learning how to walk again. It's the same with your hands and fingers and fine motor skills. You go to grab something and, instead of grabbing it, you bat it away and you have to go chasing it. You're like an infant concentrating on picking up a Cheerio for the first time.

And I felt horrible, absolutely terrible. Adjusting my body to space was unpleasant. The first thing I noticed was the fluid shift. There's lots of fluid in the human body: blood, plasma, water, mucus. On Earth, gravity keeps it in the right place. In space, it's free to float up to your head. Everybody's face was red and flushed and puffy. We were floating around, looking like puppets in a Mardi Gras parade with giant papier-mâché heads. Another physiological change that happens is that your spine elongates because there's no gravity keeping it in place. You grow about an inch in space, and all those sensitive muscles in your back have to stretch and adjust. That was uncomfortable.

Then there's the nausea. "Stomach awareness" is the official term. That whole first day, I floated around feeling like I was going to barf at any moment. Space sickness is similar in feeling to motion sickness. The effect is the same, the nausea and the vomiting, but the root cause is different. When you're below deck on a boat, you can't see the motion of the sea, so your eyes are telling your brain that you're completely still, but your vestibular system, which is located in the inner ear and senses movement, is going up and down with the waves. It's the same thing if you're trying to read in a moving car. The conflict between those two sensory inputs is what creates the feeling of nausea. In space, you're floating around and this time it's your eyes that are telling your brain that you're moving and your vestibular system that's telling your brain that you're still. Your vestibular system relies on gravity to work, so it doesn't work when you're weightless.

The more you move around, the worse it gets. You think you're going to get to space and be weightless and have fun doing flips and floating upside down, but in space there is no up or down. To your brain, floating sideways or upside down feels the same as standing right side up. So if you spin around or flip upside down, the sensation you get is not that you've spun or flipped around. What you feel is that the room is spinning and flipping around you while you're staying perfectly still, which causes the worst vomit-inducing feeling of vertigo that I have ever experienced. After a couple of days, I got used to it. I could have a conversation on the ceiling and not notice. But it takes the brain time to adapt, so at the beginning you move as slowly as possible.

One of my main jobs that first day was to help Nancy set up the robot arm and open the payload doors to deploy the radiators. The equipment on the shuttle generates heat, and the payload bay doors have radiators on them that radiate that heat out into space; otherwise, you'd cook yourself. If you can't open those doors, you're going home ASAP. I tried to ignore the nausea and focus on working with her. Everyone else was doing the same, plodding around, doing their tasks, nobody saying much. It was not a party atmosphere. It was not "Yeah! We made it to space!" It was "Ugh. Leave me alone. I'm gonna puke." That kind of sickness overcomes everything. You can be in space, you can be at Disney World, but as long as you have that grumpy, barfy, nauseated feeling, nothing is going to make life okay. I forced myself to drink a bunch of water and immediately threw it up. But after that, I felt better.

Around six hours postlaunch, the shuttle was set up and ready for our journey to Hubble. I had a bit of time to look out the windows, but not much. It was already time to go to bed. Window shades go up on the flight deck, because daybreak comes every ninety-seven minutes and you have to block out the sun. Once they were installed, we started winding down. I took off my contacts and put on my glasses. I brushed my teeth. When you rinse, you either have to spit into a towel or swallow; I swallowed. I took some anti-nausea medicine to make me feel better and make me sleepy.

My first night in space was weird. Scooter and Digger slept on the flight deck, in case we had an emergency. Other than that, you can sleep pretty much anywhere. On the ceiling if you like. John wanted to sleep in the air lock, because it's cooler in there and he likes being cold when he sleeps. I was in the mid-deck with everyone else. Everyone has a sleeping bag with clips to attach to the wall. You don't want to be floating around because you'll knock your head or wake up your friends. Then, once I got inside the sleeping bag, I was floating inside this cocoon. Once you get used to it, it's the most relaxing way to sleep ever. What astronauts also found over the years is that people like having their head against something, even if they're floating in the air, so NASA developed pillows that attach to your head with a headband.

I felt strange that first night. I've never dealt well with transition, with new things, and this was the ultimate new thing. I was out of sorts. I felt horrible. Everyone was grumpy. But then, once I was in bed—and maybe it was the anti-nausea medication—after a few minutes I started to feel better. There was something about going to bed that made me feel okay. The day was over and I had a chance to relax and reflect. I'd made it to space.

By that morning, I was hungry again. I ate a peanut butter and jelly sandwich I had left over from the day before, and once I started eating, for the next ten days I didn't stop. Eating in space was fun. All your food is pre-prepared. You don't have to cook it. Some of the food is dehydrated and you add water and heat it up. Some of the food is thermostabilized, meals ready to eat, which you just warm up as is. You select your own menu, too. Spaghetti and meatballs, macaroni and cheese, shrimp cocktail, steak, lasagna. The meals are in pouches, and you simply cut the pouch open and eat with a spoon. You have to be careful, because everything floats, but that's the fun part. Popping M&M's in the air and going after them and chomping them like Pac-Man. I actually gained weight in space, which is rare. I'm one of only two astronauts that I know of to have done so. The doctors were confounded, but I just loved eating up there.

The drinking water on the shuttle is a by-product of the fuel cells. It's actually a brilliant piece of engineering. We have tanks of liquid hydrogen and tanks of liquid oxygen. When they're combined, it creates a reaction that produces power for the fuel cells, and the by-product of that is water, which is then purified with iodine. It's much better than the drinking water system on the space station. They use solar arrays for power, which means there's no water being generated. They have some delivered, but 80 percent of it is recycled urine, sweat, and condensation collected through a filtration system that cleans it and puts it back out for astronauts to drink. As my pal Don Pettit described it: Today's coffee is tomorrow's coffee. I was glad I was going to Hubble.

By day three, we were closing in on Hubble and our main objective was to rendezvous with it, a complicated and delicate task. We were roused by the theme from *Mission: Impossible*. Wake-up was around 8:30 p.m. Houston time. Just after midnight we reached the telescope's orbit, coming in about ten miles behind it. We slowly closed the distance between us until finally we had visual contact. At first sight, the sun reflecting off the telescope looked like a distant star, another point of light among all the others. Slowly it grew bigger and bigger, taking the familiar shape I was used to: a bright silver cylinder. It was shinier than I expected. This human-made celestial object, this marvel of human engineering out in the middle of space, was an incredible sight.

The final half mile of the approach was hand-flown, with Scooter taking manual control of the shuttle, firing the engines to slow us down and make tiny course corrections. Nancy was preparing the robot arm. I was standing by as her backup and also taking photographs and video to document the rendezvous. The whole crew was tense, focused. Scooter was closing the distance between us at less than half a mile an hour. The whole thing played out like the high-tension climax of an action movie, only in slow motion. At thirty-five feet, Scooter held our position and handed things over to Nancy to grapple the telescope and bring it in.

At 3:31 a.m., over the Pacific Ocean just south of the coast of Mexico, Nancy successfully grappled the Hubble and brought it down and secured it in the payload bay outside the cabin. There was a huge sigh of relief and much rejoicing from everyone in the cabin. We were happy campers. But relief gave way to anxiety as a new thought overwhelmed me: Now that we had it, I was going to have to go out there and spacewalk on it.

On day four, we woke up to Mozart's "Five Variations on Twinkle, Twinkle Little Star." This was John and Rick's big day. Whichever spacewalking team isn't going out works as backup for the team that is going outside. You help them get dressed, check their gear, like the corner-man helping a fighter get ready for the ring or a parent getting their kids dressed to go out to play in the snow. Once the other team is outside, you and your partner take turns running the EVA checklist. The spacewalkers have enough to do without having to worry about remember-ing each and every task.

That first space walk was going to be a mirror image of what Newman and I would be doing the next day, swap-ping out a solar array. I thought it would be a good idea for me to watch them do it first and see what I could learn. Rick had the same task I did, rotating the array by hand, and it was his first space walk, too. There were a few mo-ments where it went herky-jerky on him and he had to bring it under control. I winced every time. *I'm doomed,* I thought.

As nerve-racking as it was to watch from inside, that first space walk went smoothly. The new array went on without any problems, but the hard work took a toll. After they came back in, I went to Rick. He looked ex-hausted, physically and mentally. He was drenched with sweat, his fingers and hands white and pruney from the moisture. His hair was messed up and he had red marks all over his skin from rubbing against his suit. He looked like he had been through a war and come out the other side. I asked him, "What was it like out there?"

"It was hard," he said. "Much harder than in the pool."

Some astronauts will tell you the pool is actually harder, because there's resistance and gravity and other forces to contend with. "It'll be easier in space," some say. Oh no it won't. Why? Because you're in space, that's why. Everything is harder in space.

That night, Newman and I prepped for our space walk. One of the things you do is put anti-fog on your visor. It's Joy soap, actually, the kind you buy at the supermarket; it just happens to work well as an anti-fog solution in space suits. Joy stopped making this particular kind, so NASA bought up a lifetime supply, basically every bottle available in the world. You have an applicator and you rub a thin film of soap on and then buff it. Newman and I went up on the flight deck and watched the Earth go by in the windows while we polished and buffed our helmets.

The next morning, I woke up, had breakfast. I put on my polypropylene underwear to absorb my sweat, my liquid cooling garment, the biomedical sensors the ground crew would be using to monitor my every breath. I got my drink bag ready; you can't have any air bubbles in it, so you spin it around until the bubbles are at the top and then you squeeze those out. John and Rick helped Newman and me into our suits, first the pants, then the torso, then the gloves. I went over my notes in my flight notebook, went over my checklist. The final step was the helmet. I scratched my nose one last time, gave a nod, and John carefully placed the helmet over my head, lowered it onto the neck ring, snapped it into place, and then locked it.

Inside the air lock, you go through your final checks and then you to do a forty-minute pre-breathe of pure oxygen. The air we breathe on Earth is a combination of nitrogen, oxygen, and other gases, and the air pressure at sea level is 14.7 pounds per square inch (psi). When your body moves to a lower air pressure (the pressure in the suit is 4.3 psi), nitrogen bubbles may form in your blood, which is what causes decompression sickness—the bends. The atmosphere and air pressure inside the shuttle are normally engineered to be identical to what we experience on Earth. But twenty-four hours before the first space walk, we depressed the shuttle cabin to 10.2 psi and kept it there. That made the change in air pressure less extreme. Then you do the pre-breathe of pure oxygen on top of that to rid your body of nitrogen, and that way you don't get sick.

During the pre-breathe, you're attached to the airlock wall to keep you from banging around. So, right before you're about to face the most memorable and intense moment of your entire life, you've got forty minutes to do nothing but hang there and obsess over everything that could go wrong. I tried to stay focused, going over the checklist on my cuff, thinking about my tasks, double- and triple-checking to see if everything was right with the suit. But my mind wandered. My eyes kept drifting nervously. At one point I looked at Newman and we locked eyes. He nodded at me and I nodded at him. Then I looked over at the outer hatch. I remember staring at it and thinking: *There it is. That's the door to space.*

I wonder what's on the other side.

15

EARTH IS A PLANET

When people ask me what it feels like the first time you spacewalk, what I tell them is this: Imagine you've been tapped to be the starting pitcher in game seven of the World Series. Fifty thousand screaming fans in the seats, millions of people watching around the world, and you're in the bullpen waiting to go out. But you've never actually played baseball before. You've never set foot on a baseball diamond before. You've spent time in the batting cages. You've run drills and exercises with mock-ups and replicas. You've spent months playing MLB on your Sony PlayStation, but you've never once set foot on that mound. And guess what. The Series is tied and the whole season is on the line and everyone is banking everything on *you*. Now go get 'em. That's how I felt sitting in that air lock. NASA was trusting me to do millions of dollars in repairs to this billion-dollar telescope . . . and until that moment I'd never laid a hand on the actual telescope.

I watched the clock tick down, anxiously waiting for it to get to zero. Finally it did. Once the pre-breathe was over, we unhooked our suits and we were floating. Scooter came by for a handshake and then Digger popped in for one last goodbye. During our training, as the only two rookies, Digger and I had become close. In the months leading up to the flight, we talked about dreaming about space since we were kids and what we were most looking forward to. Being weightless and looking out the window excited us the most, but I was going to get to spacewalk and he wasn't. Right before we launched, he'd come up to me and said, "Mass, since I'm a pilot, I'll never get a chance to spacewalk, but you gotta do something for me. I want you to look around out there and, as soon as you get in, I'm going to come to you and I want you to tell me what it's like. I want a description fresh from your mind. You gotta promise me you'll do that." Now he wanted to make sure I made good on my promise. "Good luck, Mass," he said. "You'll do great, and remember, I want a full report."

I told him I would give him one, and quietly I thought to myself: *I hope it's a good one.* Then John floated over to the air lock's inner hatch and pushed it closed. He pulled the handle down and spun it shut. It sounded like I was being locked in a prison cell. *WHOMP! CHA-CHUNK!* I looked over at Newman like *I guess this is it. There's no going back now.*

Newman switched our suits over to their own battery power and oxygen. Then he started to depress the air lock. After a final purge of air from the air lock, we were in a complete vacuum. There was no sound. The *cha-chunk* I heard when they locked us in, I wouldn't hear that now. I could bang on the shuttle wall with a hammer and I wouldn't hear that, either; there's no way for that sound to travel. The only noise I could hear was the sound of my internal cooling fan and some squeaking from moving around inside the space suit. My voice sounded different, too, because the sound wave travels differently through the lower atmospheric pressure. It's at a lower register. I sounded like I was about to cut a blues album.

At that point we were clear to go.

Newman pulled open the door to the payload bay and pushed the thermal cover aside. Then he went out first to make sure the coast was clear and to secure our safety tethers. He was out there for a few minutes. Finally he said, "Okay, you're clear to come out." I put my hands on the hatch frame and pulled myself through. I was floating on my back, looking up and out of the payload bay. The first thing I saw was Newman floating above me, hanging out with this grin on his face like *Check this out.*

Behind his head was Africa.

Hubble is 350 miles above Earth; astronomers wanted the telescope as far away from the planet as possible in order to have a longer orbit, see more of the sky, and be farther away from the atmospheric effects of Earth. The space station is 250 miles above Earth. From that vantage, you can't fit the whole planet in your field of vision. From Hubble, you can see *the whole thing*. You can see the curvature of the Earth. You can see this gigantic, bright blue marble set against the blackness of space, and it's the most magnificent and incredible thing I've ever seen in my life. One thing I was not prepared for was how blue it is, how much water there is.

After seeing the Earth, I looked down the payload bay at the telescope, and noticed the bright light from the sun. The sunlight on Earth is filtered through the atmosphere; it can appear bright yellow or as that golden hue you get at sunset. You get different colors depending on the place and the time of day, which in turn affects the color of objects as we perceive them. In space, sunlight is nothing like sunlight as you know it. It's pure whiteness. It's perfect white light. It's the whitest white you've ever seen. I felt like I had Superman vision. The colors were intense and vibrant—the gleaming white body of the shuttle; the metallic gold of the Mylar sheets and the thermal blankets; the red, white, and blue of the American flag on my shoulder. Everything was bright and rich and beautiful. Everything had a clarity and a crispness to it. It was like I was seeing things in their purest form, like I was seeing true color for the first time.

After taking a minute to soak everything in, I translated

up to the window looking out from the flight deck onto the payload bay to get my picture taken. The hero shot, we call it, a nice memento of your first moments of space-walking. With that out of the way, I spent the next fifteen minutes or so doing what's known as translation adaptation. When you train for space walks, you're used to moving around in the pool, where there's drag on your suit from the resistance of the water. It slows you down and makes you more stable. In space there's no resistance to any move you make, so you have to go really slow. I moved up and down the forward part of the payload bay. I did some pitch and roll maneuvers, getting a sense of how it felt. I took note of how my safety tether was moving behind me so I could make sure I wouldn't get tangled up in it.

Then it was time to go to work. The robot-arm platform was positioned right at the front of the payload bay where we'd come out. I climbed onto the top of the robot-arm platform, slotted my boots into the foot restraints, and they clicked right into place. Flat and go. Perfect on the first try. Now I was ready for Nancy to move me around. For the next twenty minutes or so, Newman and I moved about the payload bay, getting things ready. We had a foot restraint that attached to the Hubble itself, so the free-floating spacewalker could anchor himself to work on the telescope. We hooked that up and did everything else we needed to do.

While we were doing this, we entered our first night pass. The Hubble orbits around the Earth once every ninety-seven minutes. Because it's so far out from the planet, it's exposed to the sun for most of that; approximately two-thirds of the orbit is in daylight, and one-third is nighttime. We had egressed from the air lock about midway through our first-day pass, and now we were about to leave that perfect white light and plunge into complete darkness. When night comes in space, you feel it before you see it. The temperature swing from 200 degrees Fahrenheit to minus 200 degrees Fahrenheit occurs in an instant. The amazing thing is that your suit protects you from that; the temperature inside stays within a tolerable range, and you have a temperature control valve you can adjust to warm up or cool down as needed. So the 400-degree swing isn't harsh, but you definitely still notice it. The best I can describe it is it's like when you're in the ocean on a warm summer's day and a cold current rushes past and it gets you down in your bones. That's what it's like. This chill ran through me and then a few seconds later it was like somebody flipped a switch and everything went black. If the sun in space is the whitest white I've ever seen, nighttime is the blackest black. It is the complete absence of light. You have some lights in the payload bay, and you have your helmet lights that light up your work area, but you can look around you and all that white, that purity that was there, it's gone. There's nothing.

You see the stars, of course. You can see the whole universe. At night, without the sun, space becomes a magical place. In space, stars don't twinkle. Because there's no atmosphere to distort your view, they're like perfect pinpoints of light. Stars are different colors, too, not just white. They're blue, red, purple, green, yellow. And there are billions of them. The constellations look like constellations. You can make out the shapes and see what early astronomers were getting at with their descriptions. The Southern Cross was my favorite. And the moon feels like it's right there. It's not a two-dimensional white disc anymore. It looks like a ball, a gray planet. You can see the mountains and craters clearly. It feels closer than it is. You can see the gas clouds of the Milky Way. You're in the greatest planetarium ever built.

Using our helmet lights to work in the darkness, our first major task was to remove the port solar array and stow it so that we could install the new one. The photovoltaic panels and their metal frame had already been retracted and rolled up, which left this ten-foot pole sticking out of the telescope. We had to fold it up against the body of the telescope. Then Newman would disconnect the old array's connectors from the diode box, the device housed inside the telescope that translates the solar energy into electric power. Then we would remove the array, with each of us grappling it from opposite ends, him at the bottom and me at the top.

To do that, Nancy had to fly me on the robot-arm platform to the top of the telescope at the back of the payload
bay. This was tricky for two reasons. With the robot arm,
the farther it extends its reach, the more it vibrates and
starts to wobble at the far end. It's the same as how your
own arm works. When your elbow is bent and your hand
is close in to your chest, it's easy to hold something in
one place. With your arm outstretched and your elbow
straightened, it's harder to hold that same object still
without it vibrating—and I was the object on the end of
the arm being vibrated. The higher I went, the wider the
amplitude of the vibration, and the more wobbly it got. I
was petrified the foot restraints were going to give and I'd
go flying out of there . . . which wasn't possible, but the
fear was still real. I was digging my heels into the platform
as hard as I could. I was literally thinking: *Feet, don't fail
me now.*

The second problem was that the Hubble is forty-three
feet tall, which meant I was now standing nearly five stories above the payload bay—and my fear of heights kicked
in. I know that sounds crazy for an astronaut. Typically,
when you're floating above the Earth, the distance is so
vast that you lose any sense of height, which cancels out
the fear of falling. But looking back down at the payload
bay, I suddenly had a very real sense of height, like I was
hanging off the ledge of a five-story building, wobbling
out of control, about to plummet to my death below.

Rationally, I knew that was absurd. Even if my foot restraints came loose—which I knew they wouldn't—the worst that would happen was I'd float there. The rational part of my brain was saying, *Mike, you're weightless. You can't fall.* But the fearful, reptilian part of my brain was screaming, *You're too high up! You're gonna die!* And in the human mind, our rational voice doesn't always prevail. I reached out and grabbed the handrail of the robot arm platform and held on to it with a death grip so I'd be "safe." After that, I could breathe easier. I knew it didn't make any sense. I knew I was being an idiot, but having something in my hand made me feel more secure. I felt better after we got back and other astronauts told me they'd had to do the exact same thing.

Throughout the first-night pass and the second-day pass, we worked slowly and deliberately. We removed the old array, translated it back down to the payload bay, and stowed it in the carrier for the flight home. As we went to remove the new array from the carrier, we started to enter the second-night pass. Now, not only was I facing the most difficult task of the entire EVA, rotating the array into position, I was going to have to do it in the pitch-blackness of night.

I looked down and in the flight deck windows I could see the faces of my friends watching me intently and quietly rooting for me to succeed. It was the moment of truth. I was twenty feet above the payload bay, on the wobbly end of the robot arm. Other than the light from my helmet illuminating a few feet in front of me, it was completely black all around. Besides the radio and the fan circulating air inside my suit, my breathing was the only sound I could hear.

Inch by inch, I rotated the array until finally it was in the proper position. Success! In that moment, I felt the sweetest relief. I knew I still had work to do, but I'd faced the biggest challenge of the mission and pulled it off. I looked back down at the payload bay window, and the crew inside were all giving me the thumbs-up. I looked over at the telescope and Newman was smiling and pointing at me and saying, "You're the man!" I was mentally drained. I didn't want to ever do something like that again. Nancy flew me over to the telescope, where Newman and I mated the array's mast with the diode box assembly. That went off without a hitch. Then we unfolded the new array like a book and locked it into place. With that, Hubble had a new power source and a big boost added to its life and ability to explore the universe.

The rest of the space walk went smoothly. In fact, we were doing so well that we were moving ahead of schedule. At one point we ran into a question we needed Mission Control to answer, about whether or not they wanted us to test a latch on one of the telescope doors. As incredible as it sounds, I'd been out in space for nearly six hours and I'd taken only a few moments to glance at the Earth;

I'd been doing my best to ignore it in order to concentrate. Now, while Newman and I waited for an answer, I paused and took a closer look.

It was a night pass. We were over the Pacific, and everything was totally black but for the city lights on Hawaii and a few other islands below. As we came up on California, I felt a slight warmth and I knew the next day pass was coming. I looked across the country to see Atlanta all bright and lit up with everyone getting coffee and going to work, but right below me, Phoenix and Los Angeles and San Diego were still in complete darkness. I could imagine the tourists at the Grand Canyon, patiently waiting for sunrise to get their perfect golden shot.

The way we experience sunrise on Earth is so gradual. The black outside your window slowly turns to gray. You see a few glimmers of light reflecting off the buildings across the street. In space there is literally a line that bisects the Earth. On one side of it there is darkness. On the other side there is light. The line sweeps west, slowly and steadily, moving across Europe, across the Atlantic, across Florida, across Texas. I watched this line coming toward me. Then I looked past it up toward the sun. The first time I had ever seen a sun in a black sky. It looked like a big bright star against the blackness of space, a beacon to supply light and warmth for our planet. Then I looked back at the line again and realized: *The sun isn't moving. We are.*

There was a certain steadiness to that motion, the rotation of our planet, that I had never experienced before. No hesitation, no hints of any pause, but a steady motion, consistent for all eternity, with no variation.

At that moment I realized that, for my entire life, my perception of reality concerning the Earth and who we are had been wrong. Every morning you wake up and sit and have your breakfast and you watch the sun rise. You don't have any sensation of the Earth moving beneath you. You think you're sitting still as the sun rises in the east and crosses above and sets in the west. But the sun isn't moving. Yes, the sun and the solar system are flying through the galaxy at 45,000 miles per hour. But relative to you and me and the Earth, the sun isn't going anywhere. The whole way we talk about our place in the universe is wrong. "Sunrise" and "sunset" are words that don't make any sense. I thought of the song from the Broadway musical *Annie:* "The sun'll come out / Tomorrow." No, it won't. The Earth will rotate toward the sun tomorrow. That may not be as poetic, but it's reality.

Once Newman and I finished up and ingressed back into the air lock, I was not the same person I'd been when I went out. Newman did the depress, the pressure equalized, the inner hatch opened, and before I could get my helmet off, Digger was right there, like he said he'd be, waiting for me to tell him about my adventure. He wouldn't even let me get out of my suit. He was right there in my mug. "What's it like? What's it like?"

"Digger," I said, "you're never going to believe it."

"What?"

"The Earth is a planet."

"*What?*" He looked confused. "Mass, are you okay?"

"It's a *planet,*" I said. "It's not what we thought it was back home. It's not this safe cocoon, man. We're out here spinning in all this chaos. The Earth is a planet. The Earth is a *spaceship,* and we're all space travelers."

That's the truth, and that's still how I think of the Earth today.

16

MAYBE THIS IS HEAVEN

During the pre-breathe for my first EVA, I nervously eyed the door to space, pondering the mysteries waiting for me on the other side. During the pre-breathe for my second EVA, I fell asleep. Doing a seven-hour space walk is physically and mentally taxing. Here we were doing five of them back to back to back, and on the alternate days you don't get to rest; you're going all day to support the team outside. After a long, long day and a short night's sleep, Newman and I were back in the air lock, waiting to run our second marathon. So I took the opportunity to catch some rest.

My second EVA, installing the Advanced Camera for Surveys (ACS) was going to be different for a few reasons. Newman would be on the robot arm and I would be free-floating, which was going to give me more opportunity to move around like a spaceman; I was excited about that. It was also my turn to go out first and be the team leader. A motto at NASA is "Train the new guy to be your replace-ment," and that's how we ran the EVAs. Newman was still the lead spacewalker, but he'd shown me how to do every-thing and this time it was his job to observe me as I took on those responsibilities. After opening the hatch and heading out, I took a few seconds to look around. For that brief moment, I was the only human out in space. Any-where. In the universe. That felt really cool, and I took a moment to let it sink in.

Start to finish, replacing the Faint Object Camera (FOC) with the ACS took several hours, but we didn't hit any major snags and the installation was a success. Once we knew the ACS was in and powered up, we breathed a big sigh of relief. We were proud of what we'd accomplished. Maybe we hadn't walked on the moon, but that day the crew of STS-109 made a giant leap for mankind. Getting the new camera in was a huge scientific upgrade. Install-ing the new solar array had been the more difficult task for me physically, but the ACS is one of those things you can point to and say, "This is why astronauts exist. This is why we go to space. This is how we serve the public good." If the ACS did what the engineers said it would do, it was going to unlock the secrets of the universe and help us answer a lot of the big questions about How We Got Here.

There is the one thing EVA training can't do. Working in the pool doesn't prepare you for the emotions that can overwhelm you when you're actually out in space.

Newman went to fetch the FOC from its temporary stowage location so we could secure it for the ride home. I took a moment and turned and glanced over my shoulder at the Earth again. As I looked down, the thought that entered my head was *This is something I'm not supposed to see. This is a secret. I'm not supposed to be up here.* I tried to go back to my work, but I couldn't help sneaking a second look. The planet below was so beautiful that I started getting emotional. I had to look away. I was afraid I was going to tear up, and if you get water floating around in your suit, it could be a big problem. After I'd collected myself, I looked a third time. When I did, the thought that went through my head was *If you were in heaven, this is what you would see. This is the view from heaven.* That thought was immediately replaced by another: *No, it's even more beautiful than that. This is what heaven must look like— maybe this* is *heaven.*

There are so many horrible problems on Earth: war, hunger, killing, suffering. But heaven is supposed to be this beautiful, perfect place, and from up there I couldn't imagine anything more beautiful, more perfect than this planet. We might discover life in other solar systems some- day, but for now there's nothing but chaos and blackness and desolation for billions of light-years in every direc- tion. Yet here in the middle of all that is this magnificent place, this brilliant blue planet, teeming with life. It really is a paradise. It's fragile. It's beautiful. It's perfection. And we need to take care of it. You have to stop and ask yourself: What in creation could possibly be better than this?

Another way in which I was changed during that space walk was in how I think of "home." When I was a young boy living in my hometown of Franklin Square, I thought of my home as Franklin Square. That place was my world, and I thought of myself as a person from that town in Long Island. As my experiences broadened, as I went to college and I met people from other parts of the United States, I thought of myself as more of a New Yorker. As I got older and I became an astronaut, and I was working with people from around the world, I identified myself more as an American. But then after I went to space and viewed the Earth during my space walks, the meaning of home changed again. Seeing our Earth from space made me realize that the Earth is truly our home, and it's the home that everyone around the world shares. I will always be a kid from Franklin Square, and a New Yorker, and an American. I will always be all of those things. But now I think of myself as a citizen of the Earth. No matter where we are from around the world, we share it together.

Over the course of five servicing missions, only sixteen people spacewalked on Hubble. Just as the twelve Apollo moonwalkers were the only people ever to walk on the moon, the Hubble spacewalkers are the only people ever to get out and walk around at that altitude, the only people ever to see the Earth from that vantage point. I was fortunate to experience something that day that only fifteen other people in human history have ever experienced. Those first space walks changed my relationship not just with the Earth but with the universe. Forever.

The next morning, we executed our fifth and final space walk. The installation of the cryocooling system for the Near Infrared Camera and Multi-Object Spectrometer was a success, and soon the Hubble was ready for redeployment. All satellites experience orbital decay, meaning they gradually slip closer to Earth and eventually burn up in the atmosphere. So once the final space walk was over, Scooter and Digger flew us four miles farther up in order to boost Hubble's orbit and extend its life span.

On Saturday morning, we prepared to say goodbye to the Hubble. The telescope's antennas were remotely redeployed. We maneuvered *Columbia* into a position where the new solar arrays could be exposed to the sun and fully charge up; then a few hours later, the umbilical was disconnected and the telescope was switched back to its own power supply. Then, at 4:04 A.M. Houston time, Nancy used the robot arm to lift Hubble from its cradle high above the payload bay. She let go, Scooter slowly backed us off, and the Hubble was on its way. As I watched it grow distant from the window, I felt a sense of gratitude and relief. We were sending Hubble off in better shape than when we arrived: mission accomplished.

Sunday was our day off, a day to rest and recuperate, and we needed it. STS-109 had set a new record for space-walking time on a single shuttle mission. We spent a total of 35 hours 55 minutes, beating the previous record of 35 hours 26 minutes held by STS-61, the first Hubble servicing mission. By Sunday we were exhausted and ready to blow off steam.

Commanders and pilots hate the last couple of days on shuttle missions, because everyone else gets to relax, but they can't because they still have to land safely on Earth. Scooter was going around saying, "We haven't landed yet, guys! We still have to land!" while the rest of us were taking pictures, listening to music, and dancing around in midair. After months of carefully watching every calorie I ate, I was stuffing my face, eating macaroni and cheese like it was going out of style. I took pictures with my Mets jersey and some of my other personal items. That's always fun—you float the object in the air and take a picture of it, and the folks back home get a big kick out of it. We took our crew photo. We took turns doing private video conferences with our families. I did some tricks for them, like eating floating M&M's and doing somersaults in the air.

I spent most of my day off on the flight deck, floating at the window, listening to music, and staring out into space. When we first got to orbit, I was obsessed with looking at the Earth during the day, seeing the Himalayas and the Sahara Desert and all these amazing formations from 350 miles up. Out at the edge of the planet, you can see the line where our atmosphere meets the stars, and it has this bluish-greenish hue to it that's absolutely beautiful. By the end of the mission, I'd grown to enjoy the night passes more. You'd see shooting stars, meteorites burning up in the atmosphere below. You'd see fishing trawlers lit up off the coast of Japan. But the lights of the cities were the most compelling sights at night for me. You're looking at them through the atmosphere, so they have this diffuse, orangey glow to them. I'd look for the different patterns in them. Los Angeles sprawled out. New York burning like a jewel. At night, even compared to other developed countries, the whole United States is lit up like a Christmas tree, especially along the coasts. The lights are signs of life from our planet. If a visitor from another world arrived, I imagine they'd be drawn to us by our lights.

Lightning storms at night are amazing, too. You'd be over the ocean looking down on total blackness. Then lightning would flash, illuminating the features of the clouds from within. I'd see a flash, and then another flash, then another. There would be three or four of them in a row. Then a lull. Then three or four more. It was like a form of communication, like a sequence, like the clouds are speaking to each other in code.

It was good to have some time to myself to unwind.

That first flight was extraordinary, but looking back on it, I have to say it was more intense than enjoyable. Our sleep schedule was way off, waking up at ten at night and going to bed at two in the afternoon. We were always working to catch up. I recognized the feeling from Cold Lake. Everyone was exhausted and stressed out. Weirdly, after thirty-nine years of trying to get to space, part of me wanted to hurry up and get home. I wanted to get the first flight out of the way so I could come back again as a veteran. At the time, astronauts were getting four and five flights each. I said to myself, *This was just to get my feet wet. I'll be back.* I sort of discounted the experience in my mind. I took it for granted. It never occurred to me that anything would change.

Monday morning we woke up and started getting ready to go home. I wasn't particularly concerned about reentry. The biggest worry in spaceflight at the time was launch. Rockets blow up on ascent. On Hubble, our second-biggest worry, from a safety standpoint, was the EVAs. We were concerned about losing somebody on a space walk. That same vigilance didn't apply to reentry. We knew that it posed serious risks, but we felt we'd mastered it. The Russians had lost some cosmonauts on reentry with the Soyuz, but we never had. Going all the way back to Alan Shepard's first Mercury flight, no American astronaut and no American spacecraft had ever been lost coming back from orbit. The fear that gripped me on the launchpad going up—I didn't have that coming down. It never occurred to me that Scooter and Digger wouldn't get us home in one piece.

Returning from space, the shuttle normally hits the Earth's atmosphere at Mach 25, producing enormous amounts of heat and friction. Coming back from Hubble, because we were higher, we actually hit Mach 26, which means that the Hubble astronauts have flown the highest and fastest of any astronauts in the shuttle era. Since I was on the mid-deck, I couldn't see anything. I could feel it warm up a bit, but nothing unbearable. I had a bag of M&M's tethered to my seat. It was floating above me and then suddenly it fell to my lap. I felt heavy. I felt my body being pushed down in my seat, my arms and legs having weight again.

Minutes later, Scooter and Digger brought us in for a perfect landing at the Kennedy Space Center at 4:42 A.M., capping off a 10-day 22-hour 10-minute mission that covered 3,941,705 miles. Once we came to a stop, the ground crew came in and helped us out of our harnesses. When you first stand up, not only are you weak and wobbly from being in space for almost 11 days, but your spine is crunching back down to its normal height and the sensory inputs from your inner ear that weren't there before come rushing back into your brain. You have to stand up slowly, and you feel like you're going to fall flat on your face. For a while you're walking around like Herman Munster, trying to get your bearings. We hugged and took some photos and then went inside to the crew quarters, where our families were waiting.

The single best thing about coming back to Earth was seeing my family again. Gabby was eight and Daniel was six. As soon as I walked in, they ran over and gave me big hugs. The flight surgeon had stressed to us that we weren't supposed to pick our kids up since our bodies were still adjusting to gravity, but I couldn't resist. I grabbed them up and held them as tight as I could. Daniel's Little League season was about to start. I was going to be a coach, and I couldn't wait to hit the field with him. I was so grateful to be home alive.

After reuniting with my family, I went back to crew quarters to get changed into my civilian clothes. Carola went into the room with me. It was exactly as I'd left it. Everything was the same, but I was not the same. So much had happened in between. It was the first time I had to reflect in nearly two weeks. That whole time, I had been around my crewmates in close quarters, staying focused on the mission, keeping my emotions in check. But there, in my room, I started thinking about the journey I had taken, the incredible beauty I had seen. I started to cry uncontrollably. They weren't tears of sadness or even happiness, really. I was overwhelmed. It was a release of all these different emotions I'd been keeping pent up inside: the joy and the exhilaration and the feelings of childlike wonder. I sat there for ten, fifteen minutes and cried and cried and let it all out. Then I pulled myself together, took a real shower for the first time in weeks, put on my jeans, and reentered the Earth.

Out on the tarmac, the ground crew was already hard at work, taking the *Columbia* orbiter through its post-flight inspection. Soon our spaceship would go back into the Orbiter Processing Facility to be readied for its next flight, STS-107. Shuttle missions are numbered in the order they're assigned, not in the order they fly, which is why we went first despite having the higher flight number, 109. What had happened was this: The crew for 107 was assigned about six months before we were. Theirs was a routine science mission, doing experiments in the Spacehab research module in the shuttle payload bay. *Columbia* needed to be overhauled, and there were some issues that forced 107 to delay. After that initial bump, they kept getting pushed. The experiments they were doing weren't time critical, but the station assembly flights were. So those missions kept taking precedence, pushing 107 further and further back until eventually they ran up against us, the next crew assigned to fly on *Columbia*. Since Hubble was the higher priority, management looked at the flights and said, "Okay, let's swap 'em," and 107 got bumped again. NASA flipped us in the flight order. We got their spot. They got ours. We came back. They didn't.

PART 5

RUSSIAN ROULETTE

17

FEBRUARY 1, 2003

Rick Husband and I were at a dinner in honor of Leonid Kadenyuk, a Ukrainian astronaut who was flying on the shuttle, when the subject of family escorting came up. Rick was an Air Force pilot from Amarillo, a pure soul, didn't have a mean bone in his body. Neither Rick nor I had flown at that point, but Rick turned to me and said, "If I ever fly in space, the person I want to be my family escort is Mike Massimino." I told him he could count on me. A few months later, Rick was assigned to STS-96 as a pilot. Kent Rominger—we called him Rommel—was the commander. They asked me to be one of the escorts, and I immediately said yes. It was an honor for me to help Rick's wife, Evelyn, and their two wonderful kids, Laura and Matthew, deal with the difficulties of sending a loved one off on a space flight.

Everything on STS-96 went great. I enjoyed being a

family escort. It was, for me, one of the most important things I was able to do as an astronaut. Part of it is just fun. There're lots of parties. The children are excited about watching their moms and dads going into space. You get to entertain them and see the excitement of the launch through their eyes. It's also a serious responsibility. You handle the logistics, getting the family checked into the hotel and arranging their rental car, but your main job is to be there in case something goes wrong.

When Rick was assigned to be commander of STS-107 on Space Shuttle *Columbia,* he asked me to serve as a family escort again. At the time, I was going through CAPCOM training, which was taking up a lot of my time. A CAPCOM is the person in the control room who speaks directly to the crew, the liaison between the astronauts and Mission Control. I checked with the head of the CAPCOM branch, and was told I couldn't do it. I needed to be in Houston and couldn't be going down to the Cape. I was upset. Rick wanted me to be there for his wife and his kids, and I felt that should have been the priority.

I was close with several of the other people on that flight, too, and I wanted to support their mission. Mike Anderson was probably the crew member I knew the least. Like Rick, he was an Air Force pilot, also very religious, a super-nice guy. I flew with him a few times as a back seater in his T-38. Dave Brown was a Navy pilot and flight surgeon and one of my astronaut class of 1996 Sardine classmates. Dave was a bachelor, so I didn't see him around as much as I did the astronauts with kids. But he and I happened to be down at the Cape together in 1997 when they were having the wrap party for the movie *Armageddon,* so together we got to live the life of Hollywood decadence for one night, feasting on lobster and king crab legs. Kalpana Chawla was the first Indian American woman astronaut. We called her KC. She had been the astronaut office robotics liaison when I was at McDonnell Douglas, and we'd worked closely on developing the robot-arm display. She was one of the smartest astronauts I ever worked with and a pleasure to be around.

Willie McCool, 107's pilot, had the greatest name of any astronaut ever. He was a Navy pilot who launched off aircraft carriers in fighter jets in the middle of the night, but he also wore clogs and wrote poetry to his wife. He was a sensitive fighter pilot and also a fellow Sardine. One day when my son, Daniel, was up at the office with me, Willie put him in an office chair and pushed him around the hallways at top speed, playing fighter pilot. Daniel loved it. Laurel Clark was a Navy flight surgeon. Her nickname was Floral because she wore bright, flowery clothes and she had a bright personality to go along with it. Laurel was also a Sardine and she lived around the corner from me. She and her son, who's about Daniel's age, moved to Houston a few months ahead of her husband, so Carola and I ended up doing a lot of activities together with Laurel and our kids.

Other than Rick Husband, the crew member I was probably closest to was Ilan Ramon. After his reelection in 1996, President Clinton had announced that the first Israeli astronaut would be flying on the shuttle as part of the special relationship between our two countries. That was Ilan. He wasn't part of any astronaut class, but he was made an honorary member of the class of '98. There were thirty of them that year, coming in right after our class of forty-four, which meant they were going to wait a long time to fly. We named them the Penguins—the flightless birds. They'll fly when Houston freezes over.

A week before the launch, I ran into Evelyn Husband at the YMCA. I told her how bummed I was that I didn't get to be their escort, but if she needed anything to let me know. Then on January 16 they launched.

On January 31, their last day in space, I was doing a CAPCOM shift for the astronauts on the space station, Don Pettit and Ken Bowersox, who were up there with the Russian cosmonaut Nikolai Budarin. I got a call late in the afternoon from the STS-107 flight surgeon, Smith Johnston. The last thing a shuttle crew does the night before they come back is a private medical conference with the flight surgeon to make sure everyone is in good shape for reentry. Smith liked to bring on a "mystery guest" at the end of his calls to say hi and wish everyone well for the ride home. Small things like that are important for making you feel connected while you're off the planet. Smith asked me if I would be his mystery guest. Carola and Gabby were away on a camping trip with her Girl Scout troop, and I had to get home that night to help Daniel finish his car for the Cub Scouts' Pinewood Derby, which was happening first thing in the morning, but I said of course I'd be happy to do anything I could for the crew. Smith asked me to stop by around five o'clock, right about the time the crew would be in their pajamas, getting ready for bed.

The flight surgeon does his calls to space in a private room right off Mission Control. Once Smith had finished the medical updates, he invited me in. The Ku band communications antenna on the shuttle was already stowed, so it was a voice call, not video. The crew had to guess who I was. Smith made it easy. He introduced me by saying, "He's from New York and he's very tall." Laurel Clark shouted the answer: "Mike Massimino!" I could hear them laughing and cheering in the background. "How is it up there?" I asked. Laurel joked, "Oh, Mass. It's not good. I don't think you should ever come back. I'll take your spot next time."

I spoke mostly to Rick. That's typically how it is when you call the shuttle: You talk through the commander. "We really appreciate you taking time out of your day to come talk to us," Rick said. "Thanks so much. It's great to talk to you, and we look forward to seeing you when we get back." That was Rick, grateful and generous. We talked for about ten minutes, chatting back and forth. I could tell they were happy. They'd had a great flight but were looking forward to coming home. We said good night and I wished them luck. Smith signed off, and that was that. I ducked out to go pick up Daniel, totally unaware of the fact that—along with the CAPCOM who'd be talking to the crew during reentry—Smith Johnston and I were the last people on Earth who would ever speak with them.

Daniel's Pinewood Derby race was at 8:00 A.M. at his school. His car was designed like a Blue Angel F-18 with wings on the sides and Blue Angel stickers on it. Daniel got dressed in his Cub Scout uniform. Since I was an assistant troop leader that year, I was wearing my uniform, too. We drove over to the school. In the parking lot as we were walking in, we ran into one of the other fathers, Mike Lloyd. Mike was an Army reservist. He had some kind of portable radio he was listening to. He saw me and said, "Have you heard anything?"

I said, "Heard what?"

He looked down at Daniel. "Daniel, why don't you go on inside."

I told Daniel to go in and that I'd meet him indoors. Once he was gone, Mike said, "It looks like the shuttle came apart in the sky. They're reporting debris over East Texas."

I stared at him for a moment, dumbstruck. Then I ran and found a phone and called Steve Smith. He answered, "Hey, Mike! What's up?"

I said, "Turn on CNN and tell me what you see."

He went and turned his television on. I could hear the muffled sound of the TV, but Steve wasn't saying a word.

"Steve, what do you see?"

"It's an accident . . . It's bad."

"What do we do?"

"Go to the office," he said. "Now."

I ran and found Daniel and arranged for one of his friends' moms to look after him and get him home. Then I left and raced to the office as fast as I could. I felt completely helpless. I felt like I should be in Florida with the families. I needed to get to the office to hear what was going on, but at the same time I was dreading it. I wanted to wake up and find that the whole morning had been a nightmare.

When I walked in, I saw Kevin Kregel in the hallway. He was standing there shaking his head. He looked up and saw me. "You know," he said, "we're all just playing Russian roulette, and you have to be grateful you weren't the one who got the bullet." I immediately thought about the two *Columbia* missions getting switched in the flight order, how it could have been us coming home that day.

He was right. There was this tremendous grief and sadness, this devastated look on the faces of everyone who walked in. We'd lost seven members of our family. But underneath that sadness, there was a definite, and uncomfortable, sense of relief. Space travel is dangerous. People die. It had been seventeen years since *Challenger*. We lost *Apollo 1* on the launchpad nineteen years before that. It was time for something to happen and, like Kevin said, you were grateful that your number hadn't come up.

We gathered in the sixth-floor conference room, surrounded by the commemorative plaques of all the missions that had gone before. It was packed. Everyone had been called in. There wasn't a whole lot of wailing and crying. It was more quiet, somber: people sitting around in shock with blank, thousand-yard stares, trying to process what had happened. A few of our leaders got up and spoke. Ellen Ochoa, head of flight crew operations at the time. Kent Rominger, who was now head of the astronaut office. I mostly remember former astronaut Bob Cabana, who was deputy chief of JSC at the time, getting up to speak. He confirmed what we already knew, that the crew had been lost. He said, "This is a terrible day for the astronaut office. This is going to be one of the worst days that any of us will ever have in our lives. But we've got to get through it. The families are on their way back from Florida. As devastated as we are, just imagine how they're doing. The first order of business is to take care of them."

At 1:00 P.M., NASA made a public statement confirming the total loss of *Columbia* and its crew. An hour later, President George W. Bush gave a speech from the White House. At 3:20 P.M., it was announced that all future shuttle flights were suspended pending the accident investigation. We knew that would be the case, but now it was official.

18

WHY WE GO

After burying our friends, one Friday afternoon that June, Digger and I flew down to the Kennedy Space Center to say one last goodbye—to our spaceship. All through February and into the spring, search crews were walking the debris field that *Columbia* had left strewn across Texas and Louisiana. Anytime a piece of the shuttle was found, it was collected and shipped to the Kennedy Space Center. There, in one of the hangars, they had an outline of the shuttle on the floor. As the pieces came in, they were being cataloged and arranged where they belonged. If they found a piece of the fuselage, it would go here. If they found a piece of the landing gear, it would go there. Like putting together a puzzle. Some pieces were charred and twisted. Others were remarkably intact. I could stand in the middle of it and see: This was the ship that took me to space. My locker was here. The galley was there. That's the window where I listened to Radiohead and looked out at the wonders of the universe. By looking at what survived and what didn't, experts could try to figure out what happened and how the shuttle came apart.

Digger and I mostly walked around the hangar, not saying much. That was more or less the mood back in Houston as well. It was somber. It was like everyone had been punched in the gut. But life doesn't stop. While the accident investigation board conducted its inquiry, we still had a lot of work to do. Some of the astronauts were tasked with aiding the investigation. Some of us were tasked with reworking the shuttle systems to prevent future accidents. Most of us were tasked with keeping business as usual moving forward, which is what I was doing as best I could. We still had people on the space station. Don Pettit and Ken Bowersox ended up staying there an extra three months while they waited for a ride home with the Russians on the Soyuz, and I was CAPCOMing for them regularly. Future flight crews were already assigned, and even with those missions being delayed and shuffled around, we had to work on the assumption that the shuttle was coming back online eventually. So we kept training, kept doing runs in the pool. But there was no joy in any of it. It felt like everyone was going through the motions in a catatonic state.

The truth is, for me, things hadn't been going well even before the accident. My main goal was to get assigned to

another flight and get back to space. That had turned
out to be a challenge. As soon as STS-109 landed safely,
the Hubble team turned its efforts to the final servicing
mission, Servicing Mission 4. That last Hubble flight was
the flight that every spacewalker wanted. The culture
at NASA is about serving the greater good and there is
no "I" in "team" and all that, but people still have egos.
People want the chance to tackle the high-profile assignments. People want the chance to do interesting, challenging work. So as the last Hubble flight got under way, there
was some political jockeying going on. People were trying
to position themselves to get assigned.

On 109, John Grunsfeld had been the leader of our
EVA team. Shortly after we got back, he was called up to
DC for a new job, serving as NASA's chief science officer.
When the first set of development runs for the final servicing mission started up, I was included in them. Then
the second set of development runs started, and I wasn't
invited to the planning meetings. Suddenly, I was out of
the loop.

I went and talked to the head of the space walking
branch (EVA) and asked him why I wasn't being included.
He said it was because of my postflight evaluations on 109.
They weren't bad, but they weren't great either. It was a
matter of experience. As far as doing the work and ex-
ecuting my tasks, I'd done fine. But Newman and some of
the other people rating my performance said that I hadn't

shown the leadership skills to be a lead spacewalker. They said I needed more seasoning before I could be the lead spacewalker on a team. Basically, the EVA branch was saying I needed at least one more mission under my belt before taking a lead role. But the EVA plan for the final Hubble flight was the same as it had been for ours, to go out with two leaders and two first-time spacewalkers. I couldn't go back as a rookie, and I hadn't established myself as a leader. I was somewhere in the middle, which meant I wasn't going back to Hubble.

I was disappointed. I'd set my sights on going back. I wanted to be a Hubble guy. Now I was being told that I'd be better suited to go to station and get more experience there. But there was a long line of people who'd been training on station while I was working on Hubble. Before the accident, a whole bunch of station assembly flights were announced, and I wasn't on them. I was in limbo. Then *Columbia* happened and I wasn't sure if I'd ever fly again.

The *Columbia* accident was one of those situations where no one person is to blame but ultimately everyone is responsible. We had all allowed ourselves to become complacent about reentry. We were all guilty of underestimating the danger. Like most accidents, *Columbia* was 100 percent preventable. If proper safety protocols had been in place and been followed, our friends might still be alive today.

If the *Columbia* accident exposed NASA's greatest weaknesses, the recovery from *Columbia* may have been NASA's finest hour. No attempt was made to cover up the cause of the accident or deflect accountability. No question went unasked. No assumption went unchallenged. Every single aspect of the shuttle's operations was taken apart, looked at, rethought, and rebuilt. We worked around the clock for two years straight in an all-hands-on-deck effort to understand what had happened and to prevent it from ever happening again. When I look back on it now, it was truly amazing what we accomplished. That superhuman effort was enough to put the shuttle back in operation to complete the work of assembling the International Space Station. That was great, but in the end, it wasn't enough to save the shuttle program itself—and it wasn't enough to save Hubble.

On January 14, 2004, President Bush announced what he called a "new vision" for America's space program: finishing the space station, building a heavy-lift vehicle capable of taking us out of Earth orbit, back to the moon, and eventually to Mars. But this ambitious, long-term goal would require short-term sacrifice. The money to pay for it would come from retiring the shuttle in 2010 once the assembly of the space station was complete.

One week after Bush's speech, NASA made another announcement: Hubble was off the books. It was too dangerous, too risky. It was a unilateral decision. There was no discussion, no review, no panel to study the pros and cons. The backlash was immediate, and it was *big*. Across the board, nearly everyone in the scientific and aerospace community said it was a mistake.

The team at the Space Telescope Science Institute made their own case for Hubble in the best way they could. They rushed out the release of its latest images: the deepest photographs ever taken of the universe. These pictures showed the most distant galaxies ever recorded, nearly ten thousand of them, some nearly as old as the universe itself. If we wanted to continue to study them and learn more about our universe, there was only one option: Save Hubble.

Inside the astronaut office in Houston, watching these decisions being made in DC, we were devastated. Canceling the flight was out of consideration for our safety, but nobody asked us. We were still willing to go. As horrible as *Columbia* had been, the bottom line was that the accident didn't add any new information. It's not like anyone was surprised. We knew the risk was there.

For me, with *Challenger*, the danger had been more an abstraction. Now it was right in front of me and I wondered how I would react. The truth is, it didn't change anything. Carola and I had exactly one conversation about it. It was maybe a week after the accident. I asked her, "What do you think, now that this has happened?"

She said, "Well, we always knew it could. You've only flown once. Don't you want to go again?"

"Yeah."

That was the end of the discussion. Carola is a physical therapist. Every day she deals with people who headed out their front door and got in horrible car accidents and have to learn to walk again. She knows you can't hide from bad things. You just have to keep doing what you're doing. Astronauts go to space. That's what we do.

Exploration is what we do. It's a basic human need, the drive to know more merely for the sake of knowing it. Understanding what's happening at the other end of the galaxy is a path to understanding ourselves—understanding who we are and why we're here. Five thousand years ago, the Earth was small and flat and ruled by angry gods who lived on Mount Olympus. Today the Earth is a giant blue spaceship hurtling through an ever-expanding universe that's 13.8 billion years old.

That's why we go.

In April 2004, about four months after the final servicing mission was canceled, John Grunsfeld called me up from DC. He said, "Mass, I'm talking to Goddard about a robot mission to save Hubble." It was a bold idea. If it was too risky to send a crew, why not send a machine to perform the upgrades and repairs, one that could be operated from the ground? We still had the problem of deorbiting the telescope safely. We were going to have to send up a robot to resolve the issue anyway, so why not use that as a pretext to investigate and see if a robot could do more, like swap out batteries and instruments?

Someone in the astronaut office would have to lead the effort, and John told me that person had to be me. He said, "I need someone who knows robotics. I need someone who knows Hubble. Most important, I need someone I can trust. You're the only person who fits that bill." Normally, to start any new program in the astronaut office, you would call the head of the office and he or she would assign someone who was available. John wasn't going to take that chance. He was going outside the normal channels and having a specific request come from the NASA administrator that he wanted me on the project. "That's what's going to happen," John said. "So be ready."

Sure enough, a few days later I ran into Kent Rominger in the hallway and he told me I was going to work on the possible Hubble servicing mission. At the time, I was already CAPCOMing, working on contingency shuttle repairs, and leading the EVA proficiency training program. I asked which of my other duties this was going to replace. "None," he said. "Just add this to your plate. Keep doing everything else, but this is a priority."

I had a hunch what was happening: They were propping open a back door for us to get a crewed servicing mission on the books. I didn't say that out loud, but that's what I thought from the start. The plan in the meantime

was to send up a robot arm equipped with special ma-
nipulators that could dock to the telescope and perform
the repairs. I started putting together a team. My old ice-
cream-eating friend, Claude Nicollier, the Swiss James
Bond, was a veteran Hubble spacewalker and a specialist
in robotics. Ten years after he brought my display project
into NASA, I called him up and told him I had a project
for him. He signed on right away, and we were working
together again. We started doing simulations in Houston,
running tests up at Goddard Space Flight Center.

The robot mission was an interesting exercise, and we
learned a great deal from it, but the expense eventually
killed the project.

It did accomplish one vital and critical thing: It kept
the Hubble servicing team together and moving forward.
When a project gets dismantled, people disappear. They
need jobs. They go work for other companies. They move
on and start new lives and careers. If you let them scatter,
you're never going to get everybody back. All those skills,
all that knowledge and institutional memory, it's gone
forever. If you lose the team, you lose everything. With
Hubble, the day after the final servicing mission was canceled, people on the Hubble servicing team were already
looking for new jobs. We made sure that as many of them
as possible stayed put.

The robot servicing mission also brought me back to
life. After *Columbia,* for a while the job felt like nothing

but death and misery. It took me a year to enjoy being an astronaut again, and the robot mission is what made that happen. My mood changed. I had a challenge, a purpose. I was back working as a robot guy, and I was thrilled. It was right up my alley. I knew that telescope backward and forward. I liked working with the team at Goddard solving complex engineering problems. The robot mission also gave me the chance to be a leader in the office, to learn how to manage people. I realized my career wouldn't move forward if I didn't.

The whole time I was working, in the back of my mind I never lost hope that we would get a crewed mission back on the books. Then, on April 13, 2005, propping open the back door with the robot mission finally paid off. On that day, Michael Griffin replaced Sean O'Keefe as NASA administrator. Griffin was a space guy to his core. He was a former chief engineer at NASA, had been the head of the space department at Johns Hopkins University's Applied Physics Laboratory, and had done serious work at different aerospace contractors. He and Grunsfeld had been friends for years, and they both shared a love for Hubble.

Griffin was an outspoken, no-nonsense type of leader. From the second he showed up, it was clear there was a new sheriff in town. On the question of whether NASA should be focused on doing science experiments or exploring space, he didn't leave any doubts about where he stood. In one of his earliest speeches to the troops, I remember him saying, "We're not the National Science Foundation. We're NASA. We go places."

At that point the space station was close to being finished, the shuttle program was already winding down, and NASA's next big program was still years away from being operational. So Griffin decided there was one thing he could do to leave a lasting mark. A few weeks after Griffin's swearing in, John was down in Houston and he stopped by my office. "I talked to Griffin," he said. "He wants Hubble. He wants us to find a way to go back."

PART 6

WORTH THE RISK

19

FROM THE ASHES

The first time I met Drew Feustel, I thought, *This guy's gonna be a royal pain.* Drew was class of 2000, the Bugs. Shortly after *Columbia,* he was scheduled to go through space walk training, and as part of my new role in the EVA branch I was paired up with him for his first runs in the pool, the same way Steve Smith had been paired up with me. I knew how difficult the training was and I wanted to help the new guy as much as I could. A few days before his first run, I called him up and said, "Hey, you want to go out to the pool and go over some things to prepare for the run?"

He kind of blew me off. "Nah, I think I've got it."

Then, the night before the run, I bumped into him in the parking lot at the grocery store. He was sitting in his car, this classic BMW roadster, listening to music with his two boys. I said, "You want to hit the pool early?"

He shrugged. "Eh, okay. Whatever you wanna do."

I said, "Look, this is important. This is your run. I'm only trying to help."

"Yeah, yeah. Okay. I'll be there."

He wasn't there. I went in early the next morning and sat around waiting. Drew showed up late. We rushed through the briefing, and the whole time I was thinking, *This guy's gonna mess everything up. He's gonna be terrible.* Then we got in the water. He was unbelievable. My first time in the water, I struggled just to get around. Drew did everything perfectly, and the whole time he was loose and confident—a natural.

Drew Feustel wasn't your typical astronaut. He wasn't a military guy. He grew up outside Detroit and didn't have the grades to get into college, so he went to work as an auto mechanic. It turned out that while he wasn't great at sitting in a classroom, he was a genius with anything mechanical. Give him a pool pump or lawn mower, or a race car engine, and he could take it apart and fix it and put it back together better than before. While working as a mechanic, Drew graduated from community college and then went to Purdue, where he met his wife, Indi, and from there went to Queen's University in Canada, where he got a doctorate in geological sciences.

Eventually, I got to know Drew better and I saw that he was cool and laid-back and knew what he needed to do and didn't beat himself up about the small stuff. But that

took a while. For a long time after that first run, I thought
he was just cocky. I didn't know that he was one of the
greatest guys I was ever going to meet, or that our friendship would be something I'd need in order to get through
the lowest moment of my entire life.

Once Mike Griffin came on board and gave NASA the nod
to start thinking about Hubble, I started feeling hopeful.
There were quiet rumblings around the office: "Hubble's
coming back." I was getting calls from the team at Goddard, asking me what I knew and if I was going to be involved. For over a year we'd been using the robot mission
to hold the team together. Now there was a sense that we
were really going back to work. In July 2005, STS-114
flew, the first shuttle flight since *Columbia*. Everyone was
anxious. It didn't go well. The shuttle made it home safely,
but there was still foam coming off the external fuel tank.
We were grounded for another year while they continued to work on the problem. Despite the setback, we kept
moving forward with Hubble.

After 109, I was disappointed that I hadn't been upgraded to a space walk leader, and it turned out I wasn't
the only one who didn't make the cut. There were six
other spacewalkers in my class who did well on their first
flights but still weren't reassigned. We needed more EVA
leaders. Right before *Columbia*, Dave Wolf was named the

new EVA branch chief. He noticed the problem and came to me and wanted to talk about how to fix it. I suggested that we have a program to help junior spacewalkers get upgraded. He liked the idea. "Great," he said. "Why don't you head that up." That was something I learned about the astronaut office over the years: If you propose something, you'd better be ready to run it. Dave gave me an office in the EVA branch and put me in charge of putting the program together and managing it.

Then, in the fall of 2005, Dave Wolf took two months of personal leave and tapped me to fill in for him as temporary head of the EVA branch, which put me in a position to attend the astronaut office staff meetings. At one of these meetings, it was announced that Chuck Shaw, a former flight director, would be heading up a panel to explore the possibility of going back to Hubble. The rumblings were now official.

Kent Rominger had taken over for Charlie Precourt as head of the astronaut office shortly before the *Columbia* accident. Rommel was a Navy pilot, a great guy, and a strong leader during some difficult years. He and I had been close friends ever since we served as family escorts together for John Glenn's return flight in 1998. Shaw's committee was going to need a crew representative, and it was Rommel's job to name someone for it. There was a lot of jockeying around that appointment. The people who'd disappeared when Hubble was canceled, suddenly they were back, poking around, offering to help. But John and some of the other Hubble guys went to Rommel and told him, "Mass is the guy you should put on this." I had carried the flag for Hubble when it seemed there was no hope it would ever come back. Rommel recognized that. He put me and John on the panel and said, "Go to the meetings and do everything you can to help them bring the mission back on."

The main question Shaw's panel had to answer was: How do we make sure the crew gets home alive? With the shuttle at Hubble's orbit, we'd have the ability to survey the thermal protection system for damage, using the robot arm and the special inspection boom. We'd have the ability to repair that damage up to a certain point, using the different techniques we'd been developing since *Columbia*. What Hubble was missing was the space station, a safe haven in the case of a debris strike from which we couldn't recover.

The solution we came up with was a rescue mission, a second shuttle on standby on the launchpad with a crew ready to fly. The only time two shuttles had ever been on the launchpad at the same time ready to launch was in the movie *Armageddon* and that was make-believe, faked with CGI. We were officially in Hollywood action-movie territory now. If necessary, the two shuttles would rendezvous, payload bay to payload bay, link up with the robot arm, and the crew would spacewalk two by two, translating along the robot arm from one shuttle to the other.

The second question was how long we could keep the crew alive at that altitude to wait for a rescue. "Survival" was a word you heard in those meetings. Shackleton mode. How long the crew could survive came down to how long we could stretch our consumables—food, water, fuel, power. We estimated that if catastrophic damage was found on the first day of the mission, the crew could survive for twenty-one days while waiting to be rescued. But with every passing day operating at full power, that timeline would contract to closer to eleven days. Once the crew ran out of power and water, that would be it. The carbon dioxide filters would quit working, and the crew would slowly asphyxiate—they would go to sleep and never wake up.

Up at Goddard, Frank Cepollina, whom everyone called Cepi and I called the godfather of Hubble, and the rest of the Hubble team were working on the same mission from the telescope's point of view: What needed to be fixed? What was feasible? What tools would be needed? Since I'd worked so closely with Goddard on the previous Hubble mission, I served as the liaison between the two groups. In Houston, Hubble was one of many programs competing for attention. At Goddard, Hubble was their heart and soul, their bread and butter. They'd never lost hope in it, not for a minute, and they were already itching to get started. Cepi wanted astronauts. He wanted space-walkers assigned to the mission so Goddard could move ahead with testing and planning. Cepi was the kind of guy who had no problem being aggressive and pushing hard for what he believed in. I'll never forget, he came down to Houston for a meeting with Rommel and told him, "I need a crew."

Rommel said, "I can't give you a crew. You don't have a flight." And that's the way it was: We were in this strange limbo. But we never let that deter us. John and Cepi and everybody else, we kept pushing. There was a feeling that we were going to make this flight happen through sheer force of will, no matter what obstacles were put in our way.

Late November, we received authorization to start doing development runs in the pool. Rommel needed to put someone in charge of them. Again, John and the older Hubble guys recommended me. I'd dreamed of being a Hubble guy and I was honored and humbled that they now saw me as one of their own. Between the robot mission, my work on Chuck Shaw's panel, and being the liaison with Goddard, they knew that nobody was as close to that final servicing flight as I was. Rommel called me into his office and told me I was in charge of the runs. Based on the work I'd been doing and the leadership I'd shown in the office, he was confident I could be a space walk leader.

When I walked out of Rommel's office, I was in shock. To be a lead spacewalker, and possibly going back to Hubble, was at that point beyond my wildest dreams. It felt more incredible than my becoming an astronaut in the first place. Whenever I'd faced obstacles before—when I'd failed my qualifying exam at MIT or been medically disqualified by the astronaut selection board—there had always been at least a crack in the door for me to fight my way back in. But after 109 and *Columbia,* the idea of going back to Hubble . . . I felt that door had been closed, nailed shut, and painted over. I was told I wasn't good enough. I was told I wasn't going back to Hubble, that I wasn't qualified to be a lead spacewalker. Then *Columbia* happened and I hit rock bottom. But I'd worked hard and kept going. And now my hopes and dreams had been rekindled. I'd risen from the ashes, and so had NASA.

I couldn't say I was definitely going to have a spot on the Hubble flight, but I got the sense that it was mine to lose. When Rommel put me in charge of the development runs, he said, "Assume you're on the flight. Who would you want with you?" I got to pick my dream team, more or less. I brought in several veteran Hubble guys, like Joe Tanner and Rick Linnehan. I also picked a bunch of rookies who hadn't flown but whom I liked for the job. Drew Feustel was one of them. Michael Good, whom we called Bueno, was another. Bueno was an Air Force navigator, a real no-nonsense, by-the-book military type. Feustel was loose and laid-back. Bueno was solid as a rock. They were a good balance.

To fly us on the robot arm in these runs, I suggested Megan McArthur, whom I got to know when she was training to be a CAPCOM. Most astronauts apply to NASA three or four times and don't get in until their mid- to late thirties. Megan got in on her first try. She was twenty-eight and hadn't yet even completed her PhD. NASA wanted her that badly, and when I met her, I understood why. She's one of the smartest, most capable people you'll ever come across, and a terrific person to work with. Any minute with Megan is a fun minute. She became the younger sister I never had.

With those selections, we had one slot left to fill. I wanted John, but Rommel was giving me pushback. Grunsfeld had already flown several times, and Rommel was being pressured to spread things around. He had three other candidates in mind. They were all good astronauts, but they didn't know Hubble. Rommel made his case for assigning them and then asked me what I thought. I said, "If you want to go to a ball game, pick one of those guys. If you want to fix the Hubble, pick John Grunsfeld." He picked Grunsfeld. John had stuck up for me on 109, and now it was my turn to do the same thing for him. It was the right thing to do and, loyalty aside, he was the right guy for the job.

We did one set of development runs in February 2006

and another in April. In July, STS-121 flew, and it was
a great success. The insulation problems with the external tank had been fixed, the inspection protocols worked
smoothly, and the crew made it home safely. In September, STS-115 flew, and that flight went perfectly, too.
Nearly four years after *Columbia,* the shuttle program was
back. The station assembly flights were cleared to resume.
Momentum was building. Now we were only waiting for
word on when we were going back to Hubble.

In September, Steve Lindsey, who served as commander
of STS-121, took over for Rommel as head of the astronaut office. He asked for a meeting with me and John to
get an update on the servicing mission. We went into the
meeting a bit anxious. At that point, as confident as we
felt, we still didn't know if the mission would happen.
Spaceflight assignments are always tentative. Things can
change, especially when a new chief of the astronaut office comes in. Maybe the old boss had a plan, but the new
boss wants to throw it out and start over. Even after a
flight is announced, you can still be taken off it for vari-
ous reasons. Nothing is certain until the rockets light up.
That's when you know you're going somewhere.

We told Lindsey about what resources we felt we
needed and how we were addressing the risks and gave
him the whole rundown. He started talking about the
publicity that was going to be involved because of the

danger. "There's going to be a big announcement when this comes out," he said. "This is going to be the most dangerous mission in the history of the shuttle program, and the press is going to pick up on that and make a big deal out of it." He said he was telling us so we could prepare our families to start hearing that from the media.

Prepare our families? John and I must have looked a bit confused. At a certain point, Lindsey stopped and looked at us and said, "You guys do know you're on it, right?"

After the meeting, John came by my office with this big smile on his face and said, "Do you realize what just happened? He just assigned us to Hubble." For over a year we'd been working on a flight that didn't officially exist. Now we'd been assigned to a flight that hadn't been officially announced. For something like that to happen was completely outside the normal channels, but then there was nothing normal about the way this mission was coming together.

Once full flight operations resumed, things moved fast. Typically, the way NASA works is that any major decision takes a couple of months. Hubble came together in a matter of days. On October 26, Chuck Shaw went up to Washington to present his panel's findings to Mike Griffin, outlining the rescue plan and the survival strategy. That was on a Thursday. On Friday, an internal announcement was made that Hubble was back on the books. Over the weekend, calls went out to the crew.

Grunsfeld and I didn't get calls. We already knew we

were assigned. Bueno and Feustel were assigned to fill out the rest of the EVA team. Scooter was named our commander, which made me feel even better about the mission. Megan McArthur was assigned to be our robot-arm operator and flight engineer, and our pilot was Greg Johnson, nickname Ray J. Megan called him our "Ray J of Sunshine." He was always happy. Ray J is one of those Navy guys who loves to fly. For years he worked as an instructor out at Ellington, flying T-38s, where he got to love working with astronauts so much he decided to try to become one himself. It was a fantastic crew: Every single person was a person I would have picked for the job.

On Tuesday morning, October 31, Halloween, Mike Griffin held a press conference at NASA headquarters to announce the flight: STS-125 would be launching in October 2008 aboard the space shuttle *Atlantis*. The seven of us gathered in Scooter's office on the fifth floor to watch the announcement that was to be made by both Mike Griffen and U.S. senator Barbara Mikulsky of Maryland (home of the Goddard Space Flight Center). It was a big deal. We were told to be ready for a second press conference that afternoon in Houston. We called down to public affairs to try to dig up some matching NASA polo shirts. Then we went out for Chinese food and tried to process what was going on. We were floating on air without even launching off the planet.

Normally, to announce a flight, NASA would just send

out a press release. Then, once the crew was assigned, another press release would go out a few months later. We typically didn't talk to the media until L-30, thirty days out from launch, and even then, the coverage was mostly perfunctory. This was unprecedented. I don't recall any other occasion when the flight and the crew were announced simultaneously with so much fanfare or with so much attention given to the crew. Shuttle crews are usually nameless: a team, a unit. But at our press conference that afternoon, all seven of us did a Q&A from the front of the room, and then they broke us out for one-on-one interviews. NASA was really putting us out there. I sat with reporters so long I almost missed trick-or-treating that night.

20

ONE LAST JOB

Because this was going to be the final trip to Hubble—
ever—we had a long checklist of tasks we needed to
accomplish. As always, our first job was to repair and
refurbish the telescope's existing equipment to keep it
working: replace the batteries, replace the gyros. These
improvements would take the failing, dying telescope and
give it anywhere from five to ten years of new life. We also
planned to add a fixture to the bottom of the telescope
that would allow an unmanned rocket motor to fly up,
dock with the telescope, and guide it down to safely burn
up in Earth's atmosphere when it was finally time for the
Hubble to retire.

We also planned to give the telescope two major upgrades. The first was to remove the Wide Field Planetary Camera 2 (WFPC2) and replace it with the Wide
Field Camera 3. The WFC3 was going to be Hubble's first

panchromatic camera, able to observe across the ultra-violet, visible, and infrared spectrums. Young stars and galaxies burn bright in the ultraviolet range, while dying stars and older galaxies emit light only on infrared wave-lengths. By spanning that range, the new camera would allow us to observe the evolution of galaxies and see fur-ther back in time than ever before. The second upgrade was to install the Cosmic Origins Spectrograph, or COS, which was going to measure and study ultraviolet light emanating from faint stars and distant celestial objects, allowing us to study the large-scale structure of the uni-verse and the ways in which planets and stars and galax-ies are formed.

The public loves the incredible images we get from Hubble's cameras, but for scientists, spectography is a vital part of the telescope's utility. Which is why the sin-gle biggest, most worrisome task of the mission was re-pairing Hubble's other spectrograph, the Space Telescope Imaging Spectrograph (STIS).

STIS was installed on Servicing Mission 2 in 1997 and had stopped working in August 2004 due to a failed com-ponent in its low-voltage power supply board. It had been resting in "safe mode" ever since. STIS allows us to study the relationship between black holes and their host gal-axies. When it was working, STIS allowed us to examine dying stars to understand what happens to them and why. Most important, it enabled us to study the atmospheres of distant planets with the hope of finding other places in the universe that are capable of sustaining life.

We needed to get STIS back.

Typically, with Hubble's scientific instruments, we never repaired them. We simply swapped the old for the new. That alone was challenging enough. But we had no replacement unit for STIS and no budget to build one. We did have room in the budget to try to repair it. There was only one problem: STIS was never meant to be repaired. It wasn't designed to be opened up. By anyone. Ever.

The power supply we needed to replace was housed behind an access panel about fourteen by twenty-six inches. Holding that panel down, in the top left corner, was a metal clamp held in place by two torque-set screws. A handrail that was used for installing and removing the instrument was also blocking the panel. It was held in place by four hex-head screws. The clamp and the hand-rail and the six screws holding them in place all had to come out.

The screws we needed to remove from the clamp and handrail weren't magnetized, so they weren't going to adhere to the drill bit when we pulled them out; there was a good chance they'd go flying off. Also, each of these six screws had a washer behind its head. When we pulled the screws out, those washers would float off, too. In addition to the washers, to make sure these bolts never, never, never came loose, the threads of each screw were covered with glue. They were literally glued into place. When we pulled these screws out, microscopic bits of dried glue would come flaking off and float away as well. And since astronauts are working with oven mitts in zero gravity and half the time in complete darkness, grappling with microscopic bits of floating debris is close to impossible.

And we haven't gotten to the hard part yet.

Assuming the clamp and the handrail came off clean, the panel housing the power supply was held in place by 111 very tiny screws. The reason it had so many was to keep the STIS from overheating; each screw acted as a mini radiator, allowing heat to escape and dissipate into space. Which was a rather brilliant engineering solution to the problem of regulating the instrument's temperature, but it was a design you'd use only if you never planned to open up the instrument ever again. Every one of those 111 very tiny screws also had a washer that could go flying loose, and the threads of every one of those 111 very tiny screws were also glued in place. If that weren't bad enough, 2 of those 111 very tiny screws were covered up by a metal plate. When we move things in space, it's helpful to know where the center of gravity of the object is because that's the point we want to rotate the object around. To help us, the engineers who designed STIS put a label, a metal plate, marking where the center of gravity on the instrument is. Only now that metal plate wasn't helping us. It was in the way and it had to be sheared off, also without creating any debris.

Then, assuming we could remove the clamp, the handrail, the metal plate, and the 111 very tiny screws, the four sides of the panel were sealed shut by a rubber gasket that had to be peeled loose. Then, once we peeled that loose and made sure no bits of dried rubber gasket were floating around, the panel was still connected to the instrument by a grounding wire. The grounding wire had to be cut without causing any electrical problems. Then, once that wire was cut, we would finally have access to the power supply itself. The power supply was a flat card, about nine by fourteen inches. It looked like any motherboard you'd find inside a computer, and it was held in place by channel locks, also known as launch locks, designed to protect the power supply from the violent shaking that goes along with launch. A launch lock consists of a long screw that, as it's driven in, forces the metal plates holding the board to sandwich together and clamp down tight.

Then, assuming we successfully made it through the clamp, the handrail, the metal plate, 111 very tiny screws, the rubber gasket, the grounding wire, and the channel locks, we still had to remove the failed power supply board, which was seated with a 120-pin connector at the back. We had to slide that board out perfectly straight, making sure that none of these tiny metal pins broke off inside the instrument. Then we had to slide the new power supply in—again, perfectly straight—making sure every single one of the 120 tiny metal pins went in flush. If even one of them bent or broke, the whole repair would be blown. Everything up to that point would have been for nothing.

It was like cracking a foolproof safe.

So how do you crack a safe that can't be cracked when you're 350 miles up in space?

The easiest part, hands down, would be removing the handrail. It took up a single, short entry in our check-list. Line 28: "Disengage handrail fasteners (four)." We were nervous about the 111 very tiny screws, which were hard to work with. But the handrail had four big hex screws with large interfaces, easy to engage. Piece of cake. Nothing to worry about. Removing the clamp would be slightly more complicated but also straightforward. We had a clamp removal tool specially designed to help pry it off and capture the screws as they came loose.

To deal with the 111 very tiny screws, we designed a fastener capture plate that would fit with an airtight seal on top of this panel. The plate was made of metal, about a quarter inch thick, with clear plastic compartments that had small holes in them that lined up squarely with each of the very tiny screws. Each hole was big enough to allow a small drill bit through to drive the screw out, but small enough that the screw and the washer and the flaking

glue debris couldn't escape. The plan was to go methodi-
cally, tiny screw by tiny screw. When we were done removing them, the debris would be safely contained. For
the two screws covered by the metal label, the fastener
capture plate had a built-in blade that, with a turn of a
knob, would shear the metal off, exposing the two screws
underneath.

The trick would be attaching the capture plate to the
panel itself. To do that, we had to remove 4 of the 111
very tiny screws from the panel to give us holes where we
could drive in guideposts, stanchions, to bolt the capture
plate in place. Since those four screws would be coming
off before the capture plate was attached, we needed a
way to capture the screw and the washer and the dried
glue. Each one had to be removed using a capture bit,
a special bit on the end of our power tool that grips the
head of the screw with teeth and captures it. Once we
pulled the trigger to remove the screw, it would remain
attached to the capture bit and we would carefully stow it
and move on to the next one.

That still left the issue of the washer, which could
still go flying. The plan was to insert a washer retainer,
a split ring, that could be pushed over the screw head
and snap into place around it. When the screw came
out, the washer retainer would hold the washer in place.
Then we would use a washer extraction tool to remove
the washer and the washer retainer, clearing the way for

me to insert the guide studs for the capture plate. Once the capture plate was attached, we'd drive the remaining 107 very tiny screws, remove the panel, peel off the rubber gasket, cut the grounding wire, swap the old power supply for the new, and finally install a new cover panel. The replacement cover was simple. It worked as a radiator without needing 111 very tiny screws. It simply had two levers to be pushed and locked into place. Thank goodness for small favors.

When the flight was assigned, it was assumed that John would lead three space walks, and I would be leading the other two. Drew was partnered with John, and Bueno with me. Per John's standing pronouncement about Hubble, the telescope knew we were coming to fix it, so new things started to break. Three months after we were assigned, the Advanced Camera for Surveys suffered an electronics failure that rendered two of its three channels inoperable. The ACS, like the STIS, needed to be opened up and given a new power supply, something that also was never intended to be done. This repair was at least simpler; accessing the inside of the instrument required the removal of 32 screws instead of 117, using a similar capture plate mechanism. Now that repair had to be developed and planned and added to the EVA schedule as well. After everything shook out, John and Drew were assigned the WFC3 installation, the COS installation, and the ACS repair. Bueno and I were assigned the STIS repair and the replacement of the Rate Sensor Units (RSUs) that housed the six gyros. Each team was assigned to handle one of the battery module replacements and a few other miscellaneous repairs.

I was glad that Bueno and I got the STIS repair job. I wanted it. I'm not supposed to say that. I'm only supposed to talk about the team and how I was happy to play my part and all that, but if I'm being honest, I have to say that I wanted that job as much as I've ever wanted anything. My feeling through all of this, since I was tasked with the robot mission, was that this flight was a date with destiny. All the challenges and obstacles I'd faced in life had brought me here, and the STIS repair—if we pulled it off—would be the most intricate, delicate, and complex task ever undertaken by a spacewalker. It was an opportunity to do something that had never been done in space before.

STIS repair was such a difficult undertaking that the Hubble engineers built us our own model STIS to practice on in Houston, separate from the replica at Goddard and the mock-up in the pool. We had a special room across the hall from our office that we called the Annex, and we kept the model STIS in there along with space suit gloves and a full set of tools. Every moment of free time we had, Bueno, Drew, and I would be in there practicing. It was my job to do the intricate work of performing the repair while Bueno supported me, and Drew ran the checklist.

I don't know how many run-throughs we did. We must have done it hundreds of times: Remove the clamp. Drive the guide studs. Remove the handrail. Attach the fastener capture plate. Over and over and over again.

Bueno was my EVA partner, but Drew was the guy in my ear. He and I went through something of a mind meld. He'd tell me what to do, and I'd do it. It was like we had one brain. We developed our own language. This repair was so intricate and so complicated that every item on our checklist had to be broken down into a half dozen micro-steps that all had to go perfectly. There was zero margin for error. Drew would give me verbal cues from our annotated checklist, and I would execute. Then we'd do it again and again and again. A true friendship developed. I came to realize that I'd been completely wrong about him when we met. His breezy attitude came from his confidence and natural ability, but he was dedicated and conscientious and I knew he'd have my back 100 percent if anything went wrong.

Everyone at NASA was behind us. Mike Griffin told us if we needed anything—*anything*—we were to call him directly. The support we had from the Hubble team was unbelievable. Whatever we needed, we got. We needed helmet cameras that worked in the pool. We got them. They developed them for us. We needed a lighter power tool. They built us a brand-new one just to shave a pound off the weight. We needed a new mini power tool to handle those tiny screws. They built us that. All told, we had over a hundred new tools designed and built specifically for the STIS repair alone. We were back in the Apollo days: Spare no expense, make it happen.

The media and the public picked up on the excitement surrounding the flight: We were in a race against time to save the most important scientific achievement of the modern space age. ABC News, the Discovery Channel, producers from *Nova* on PBS, they all asked to shadow us during our training to document the mission.

But the media request that turned out to be the biggest deal of all was one that I didn't even understand at the time.

Social media, especially Twitter, was just taking off. People were sending out 140-character status updates about what they had for dinner and such. President Obama had tweeted during his inauguration and apparently it was becoming the thing to do. About a month before we launched, NASA's public affairs office approached me about being the first astronaut on Twitter. They wanted me to send out updates about our training and then send the first tweet from space.

I was happy to give it a try, but I had no idea what it would turn into. I also had no idea what one was supposed to tweet about, so I just started telling people what I was doing. On April 3, we were at Kennedy for our Terminal Countdown Test, and I sent my first tweet:

In Florida, checking out our spaceship "Space
Shuttle Atlantis."

That was it. When we got back to Houston, I started
sending out updates a couple of times a day:

In a simulator practicing for the first spacewalk on
my mission

In a space shuttle simulation with my crew
practicing our rendezvous with the hubble space
telescope.

Practicing closing the big doors on the hubble
space telescope with spacewalk instructors Tomas
and Christy.

I sent out tweets from the Neutral Buoyancy Lab (NBL),
from the shuttle simulator, from Daniel's Little League
games, from Gabby's dance performances. I started following other people, and they started following me. They
had tons of questions, and I tried to answer as many of
them as I could.

With every retweet and every answered question,
the number of people following me grew—ten thousand,
then twenty, then fifty, then one hundred thousand, two
hundred thousand. And that was in less than a month, all

of them everyday people curious about the behind-the-scenes life of an astronaut. When I climbed into my T-38 and flew in formation down to Florida for launch, I was able to share that with them. When I went through the final fit check with my pressure suit and survival gear, they could be right there in the room with me. And at 2:01 P.M. on May 11, 2009, when *Atlantis*'s engines fired and that giant science-fiction monster reached down and grabbed me by the chest and hurled me into space, every single one of them got to come along for the ride.

21

LINE 28

From orbit: Launch was awesome!! I am feeling
great, working hard, & enjoying the magnificent
views, the adventure of a lifetime has begun!

That's what I tweeted once *Atlantis* reached orbit—the
first tweet from space. I continued sending tweets when
I could, bringing people along for the journey; but I was
busy from the jump, busier than I had been on 109. I was
in charge of the post-insertion checklist, converting the
shuttle from a launch vehicle to a spaceship. Fortunately,
I didn't get sick this time and was able to get everything
done. We also had to perform the inspections that, post-
Columbia, were now a standard part of our postlaunch
procedure. On day three, Megan successfully grappled
the telescope and berthed it in the payload bay while
John, Drew, Bueno, and I inspected our EVA suits, went
over our checklists, and prepared to go outside.

For the first space walk, John and Drew removed the old Wide Field Planetary Camera 2 and replaced it with Wide Field Camera 3, equipping the Hubble to take large-scale, detailed photos over a wider range of colors than ever before. They replaced the Science Instrument Command and Data Handling Unit that had failed the previous September, restoring the telescope's communication capabilities, and finished up by installing the Soft Capture Mechanism on the bottom of the telescope.

On the second space walk, Bueno and I had to swap out one of the failing batteries and install the Rate Sensor Units. While Bueno was working on those, I started on some get-ahead tasks to help John and Drew repair the ACS the next day. To get the camera working, we had to reroute power around it, using what is called a PIE harness, a cable about six feet long. From where we were positioned to work on the RSUs, I was in a good spot to set this cable up for the next day's work. I went and retrieved it and hooked it to my mini workstation so I'd have it for later.

The next thing I knew, out of the corner of my eye I saw the PIE harness floating away. Somehow the hook that I'd used to secure it had come undone and it was drifting off into space. The first thought to flash through my mind was: *That's the only one we have.* Sometimes we carry spares, like with the RSUs, but there was no spare for this harness. If it goes, that's it. There's no fixing the

ACS without it, and we're never coming back here again. I wasn't watching a harness float away—I was watching the future of astronomy float away.

I was inside the telescope, right next to the star trackers and the super-delicate instruments we're not supposed to ever bang into or disturb, but I couldn't let that harness get away. It was already about five feet above me and going fast. I lunged for it. If I hadn't been tethered to a handrail, I would have been launching myself into space, too. But I knew I was tethered. I knew it instinctively, thanks to my years of training. I didn't even double-check before jumping. I leapt up, grabbed the harness, then grabbed my tether and pulled myself back down. John was watching me from inside, and it scared the dickens out of him. He yelled over the comm, "Mass! Watch out!" The whole episode was over in seconds, and everyone at Mission Control was so focused on fixing the RSUs that nobody else took note of the fact that I had nearly ruined a key part of the mission.

We completed the RSU swap, and the new battery went in with no problems. The next day, John and Drew installed the Cosmic Origins Spectrograph and performed the Advanced Camera for Surveys repair. We were watching that repair closely because it was a dress rehearsal for the STIS repair. If John encountered any problems, he might tell me what kinds of challenges I was going to face tomorrow. But there wasn't a single glitch. Both the COS installation and the ACS repair came off flawlessly. It was as close to a perfect day in space as you can get.

I wanted a perfect day. Every pitcher wants to throw a perfect game at least once. As I sat up that night polishing and buffing my helmet, that's what I was thinking. For five years, ever since the day John called me about a possible robot mission, I'd thought about nothing besides that telescope. Now I was getting ready to go out there. I knew this would be my last space walk on the telescope. I figured there was a good chance this would be my last space walk ever. And I was about to undertake the most complex and delicate operation attempted on any space walk ever. This wasn't a run in the pool. Everything had to go right.

We woke up that morning to my song: Billy Joel's "New York State of Mind." Bueno and I started our routine, eating breakfast, putting on our garments, going over our checklists. The whole time I was thinking, *This is it. This is the day.* I knew this day would have a story to it, that it would have a beginning and an end. I didn't know how it would end. I just knew it would be significant one way or another, a day to remember. And it was. Since that day, in every speech I've ever given, I speak about that day.

We were attempting something in space that had never been done before. How were we going to do it? *Could* we do it? The reason we run through these tasks so many times on the ground is not simply to learn how to do the job right but to find out everything that might go wrong. Depending on the complexity of the space walk, so many potential problems can occur. The last thing you want is to encounter a problem you didn't think of or hadn't prepared a solution for. But you inevitably do. Hopefully, they only come at you one at a time.

The Hubble was at the back of the payload bay. I wasn't looking forward to getting back there. As the free-floater, going back and forth was always a bit hairy, because you're on the sill of the payload bay, looking over the edge into space, and you feel like you could flip and get out of control and go flying off. You're tethered to the ship, but the length of that tether is fifty-five feet, which is a long way to tumble into space before it catches you. The fear is hard to shake.

Since my space walks on STS-109, one thing had changed. The robot arm had always been berthed on the port side of the shuttle, making it difficult to translate along that path. There are some handrails, but it's tough to get a solid grip in a few places. We'd always gone down the starboard side, which had a clear path with handrails all the way down. Now we had the new inspection boom added after the *Columbia* accident. It was stored on the starboard side, and I couldn't go that way anymore. I had to pick my way along this treacherous path around the base of the robot arm, holding on to a hose here, a screw there, always worried I was going to lose my grip and

careen out of control. Part of the reason I wanted everything to go perfectly was because I wanted to go out to
the telescope once at the beginning and come back once
at the end. I wanted to spend the day back in the cocoon
of the telescope, where I could concentrate on my job.

Once Bueno and I got to the telescope, Drew started
walking us through our checklist and we were knocking
off the steps. We were even a bit ahead of schedule. I attached the clamp removal tool. That went fine. I attached
the handrail removal tools that would capture those bolts
and washers as they came off. That went fine, too. Then
I had to remove the four screws that would allow me to
drive in the guide studs that held the capture plate. These
were the four screws that stood the greatest chance of
throwing off debris that might FOD (foreign object debris)
the telescope. Slowly, very slowly, I took the drill with the
washer-retainer bit and removed the first screw. It came
out clean. Then the second. Then the third. As I came to
the fourth, I looked at it and thought, *One more of you and
I can check you off and never deal with you again.* That's
how I felt with every little thing ticked off the checklist:
I'm done with that. Never again.

The fourth bolt came out clean. Now, before I could
drive the guide studs, I had to remove the handrail. I was
using the large pistol-grip power tool I'd used plenty of
other times—nothing unfamiliar about it. The two top
screws came off, no problem. The bottom left came off,

no problem. One more and I was done. I engaged the bottom right screwhead with the tool and pulled the trigger like I'd done a thousand times before. It spun and spun. It gave me a red light. I wasn't getting a good green torque light. The drill bit was going round and round and nothing was happening. Something was wrong. I looked inside the little window of the handrail removal tool and I didn't see a hex head screw anymore. I saw a deformed, rounded thing that I'd created because I'd stuck the tool in there and pulled the trigger and ground down the screwhead.

I stared at what I'd done. *That screw is destroyed,* I thought. *It's never coming out, which means there's no way to get the handrail off, which means there's no way to get the guide studs on, which means there's no way to get the capture plate on, which means there's no way to get the 111 screws out, which means there's no way to get the old power supply out, which means there's no way to get the new power supply in, which means the STIS is broken forever, which means there's no way to discover life on other planets.*

And I'm to blame.

All of this went through my head in a matter of seconds. I looked over at Bueno. He was giving me this wide-eyed look like, *What now?* I actually had the thought, *Hey, maybe Bueno can fix it.* But I knew he couldn't take over the repair. He was my partner, but the damage was already done. I looked back at the cabin. My crewmates were in there, but none of them had space suits on and they couldn't come and bail me out, either. Then I looked down at the Earth. *There are seven billion people down there,* I thought, *and not one of them can help me.* No one can help me. I felt this deep sense of loneliness. It was an alone-in-the-universe type of alone. I felt separated from the Earth. I could see what they would be saying in the science books of the future. This would be my legacy. My children and my grandchildren would read in their classrooms: We might have known if there was life on other planets, but Gabby and Daniel's dad broke the Hubble.

I tried the pistol-grip tool again. I was bearing down hard to try to get traction and catch something to spin this screw. I'm a big guy, and by bearing down that hard, what I was also doing was pushing with my feet and putting all that force in the opposite direction into my foot restraint, which was attached to the base of the telescope. There are limits to the amount of force that fixture can take. Looking back on it, I'm surprised I didn't rip the thing right out and put a hole in the side of the telescope.

No matter how bad things appear, *you* can always make them worse.

I was making it worse. Drew came over the comm and told me to stop. "Mass," he said. "Don't. Pull. The. Trigger."

We all froze for a moment, not knowing what to do. Hundreds of test runs with an identical screw and an identical power tool had never once resulted in a stripped screw. We discovered later, during an investigation, that the problem was the staking, the glue put on the threads to hold the screws in place. This one screw had more glue on it than the other three. So when we calculated how much torque it was going to take to unscrew the screw from the handrail, we were off. If I'd been using a manual ratchet, I would have felt the extra resistance better and adjusted. But I was using this big, bulky tool set at 60 rpm, the fastest setting, and it didn't have as much feedback. Which in hindsight was not a good idea. There was no reason to do it like that. But everyone was so concerned with the 111 very tiny screws on the panel. Those were the ones we were worried about stripping. The big screws with the large interface, they were nothing. They hadn't even been a topic of conversation.

Some technician back in the mid-1990s had accidentally put a tiny extra dab of glue on the threads of that screw. I didn't know that at the time. I just felt like I'd messed up. And at that point the origin of the problem didn't matter. Even if it wasn't my fault, it was still my responsibility.

We had a backup plan if we couldn't break torque: Go in with a manual wrench and crank it loose. But we had no plan for a stripped screw. The checklist was useless. Tony Ceccacci, our flight director, was at that moment marshaling everyone in Houston and at Goddard to work the problem. Dan Burbank, our CAPCOM, was relaying their ideas to Drew, who'd then pass them on to me.

The only idea coming up from Houston was to keep trying different tools and drill bits to get that screw out, and the tools they wanted me to try were in the toolbox at the front of the payload bay—all the way at the end of the treacherous path on the port side of the shuttle. Bueno couldn't fly up there on the robot arm. The free-floater had to do it—I had to do it. I couldn't say I was scared, but I was. I started picking my way along that sill to get to the toolbox, and over the side of the shuttle I could see the beautiful Earth, only it didn't look beautiful to me. It hadn't changed, but my attitude had. As I made my way up to the toolbox, the doubts and fears that had plagued me for years—doubts and fears that I'd thought I'd put to rest—they all came creeping back. Why did I mess that up? Maybe John should have been doing this and I should have stuck to the basics. Maybe I wasn't good enough to spacewalk on Hubble in the first place. Maybe I was a bad choice, and that's what the postflight investigation would say: "It was Massimino's fault."

As beautiful as that view was, I didn't care. I didn't care about anything at that point but fixing what was going on. Then I realized that, as bad as I was feeling, being scared and full of doubt wasn't going to help. If I didn't fix this, it was never getting fixed. I got to the toolbox, fetched the tool they wanted me to try, and went all the way back. That didn't work. "Try this one." I went all the way back to the toolbox, fetched the next thing, then came all the way back again. That didn't work, either. Then it was "Try that one" and "Try this other one." I must have gone up and down the sill of that payload bay eight or nine times, fetching different tools. With every pass I lost more hope, and I didn't have much at the start. I knew the repair backward and forward, and I knew there was no way to recover from this. We were grasping at straws. We could keep trying different drill bits, but there was nothing wrong with the bit I was using. The problem was the screwhead. We kept trying things and I kept fetching tools and nothing was working.

I felt like I was living a nightmare. Very soon we were going to run out of time. I'd been going back and forth and trying different tools for over an hour. We were in a night pass when I stripped the screw, and the day-night cycles were passing. I knew that time was ticking down and they couldn't keep us out there forever. Ultimately, it was the flight director's call. I knew he was watching the clock, watching our biometrics, and doing the math. Bueno and I could get more oxygen if we needed it, but our CO_2 filters were filling up. Eventually, they'd hit their limit. Typically, we plan to be out for six and a half hours max. You can stretch it to seven, but you can't go much longer than that. People start to make mistakes from fatigue. Your life support starts to run out.

As the clock ticked down, every minute we were getting closer and closer to Bingo time.

Then Burbank came over the comm and said that they were working on something and I needed to go to the toolbox and get vise grips and tape. Tape? Seriously? I didn't even know we had tape on the shuttle. I translated back up to the toolbox at the front of the payload bay and started digging around for tape. It was dark. I was not happy. I was completely demoralized. At that moment, I was as low as I had ever been in my life.

Out of the corner of my eye, I could see Drew trying to get my attention from the flight deck window, maybe ten feet away from me. I didn't want to look up. I didn't want to talk to anyone. I didn't want anyone to see how upset and ashamed I was. Finally, I looked up, and Drew had this huge smile, almost like he was laughing. I couldn't say anything, because the ground crew would be able to hear it, so we had to communicate with gestures and facial expressions, like a game of charades. I shot him a look. *What's with you?*

You're doing great, he mouthed back, giving me a big thumbs-up.

I thought, *What is he talking about? Is there some other space walk going on right now that I'm not aware of? Because the one I'm involved with is a total disaster.* But Drew kept smiling. He started rocking his thumb and pinky finger back and forth, pointing between the two of us as if to say, *It's me and you, buddy. We got this. You're gonna be okay.*

If there was ever a time when I needed a friend, that was it. And Drew was right there, just like I'd seen in *The Right Stuff,* the camaraderie of those guys sticking together. I'd been feeling stranded and all alone, but I'd forgotten that my team was right there with me—my crewmates and everyone at NASA on the ground. If this day kept going south, no one was going to point the fin- ger at me and say, "Massimino did it." We would fail or succeed together, and that's the way it should be. Now, I did not believe Drew for a minute that everything was going to be okay. I still thought all was lost. But I did think, *Hey, if I'm going down, at least I'm going down with my best pals.*

It was at that moment that Burbank radioed in to tell us what was going on with the vise grips and the tape: They wanted me to rip the handrail off. The thought of doing something like that hadn't occurred to me; it ran counter to everything I'd ever been taught about the telescope, which was to treat it as gingerly as possible. But while I was running back and forth like a crazy person trying to fix the problem, Jim Corbo, a Goddard systems manager working out of Houston that day, started wondering if it was possible to yank the handrail off. He called Goddard and spoke with James Cooper, the mechanical systems manager for the telescope. It was a Sunday. Only a handful of people were working, but Cooper and Jeff Roddin and Bill Mitchell and the Hubble team up there started running around, trying to rig up a test to see if this would work. In less than an hour, they had the backup handrail from the clean room hooked up to a torque wrench and a digital fish scale to measure how many pounds of force it would take to break the handrail loose with one screw holding it in.

They did it. Successfully. They called Corbo in Houston with the results. Now Ceccacci and his team had to decide whether or not to give this a shot. If we didn't get the handrail off, the worst case was that the STIS stayed broken but everything else worked fine. But if we yanked the handrail off and debris got loose inside, it might destroy the telescope, compromise the mirror. Also, in space, flying shrapnel is a bad idea generally. What if I yanked the handrail off and it kicked back and punctured my space suit? Then this might become a matter of life and death.

Ceccacci decided to go for it. It was a gutsy call. But like everything else with Hubble, it was worth the risk. Burbank radioed up and explained it to us. "This was just done," he said, "just now, at Goddard on a flight equipment unit, and it took sixty pounds linear at the top of the handhold to fail the single bolt in the lower right position at the bottom."

Drew said, "Okay. Mass, you copy that? Sixty pounds linear at the top of the handrail to pop off that bottom bolt. I think you've got that in you."

I knew I had it in me. I was a big guy in the best shape of my life. I was nervous about damaging the telescope, but for the first time since the whole problem started, I felt this surge of confidence and hope.

The reason for the tape, I now learned, was to tape up the bottom of the handrail to try to contain any debris that might go flying. I made my way back to the telescope, and Bueno and I taped the handrail up. The whole time Drew, Bueno, and Burbank and I were talking this through. We decided I should start by rocking it back and forth, give it a few tugs to yield the metal a bit, and then give it one clean yank once the metal started to give. If I tried to do it in one go, all that power would be in one motion and it would snap, and debris might go flying everywhere.

Right as we got the handrail taped up and were ready to go, Mission Control called up to say they'd lost the downlink from my helmet camera and wouldn't have any video for the next three minutes. I didn't want to waste another second. And if they couldn't see what I was doing, even better. Let's have the party now while Mom and Dad aren't home. "Drew," I said, "I think we should do it now."

He said to go for it. "Just real easy, okay?"

I took a breath, braced my left hand and my feet, and looked at this handrail in front of me. When I was growing up back in Franklin Square, there was one day when I was outside throwing my ball against the front steps, and my uncle Frank came over. This was my uncle who lived across the street. He was covered in oil and grease. My dad came out, they disappeared inside the house for a minute, and then they came back out. My dad had this giant three-foot-long screwdriver with him, and he said, "Stop throwing that ball. Come across the street and maybe you'll learn somethin'."

I got up and followed them. Uncle Frank had his car, a 1971 Ford Gran Torino, parked in the street out in front of his house with the hood open. Some mechanic had screwed the oil filter in too tightly. Uncle Frank had practically destroyed the filter trying to get it out, and now it was stuck. It was a physics problem, the same problem currently staring me in the face 350 miles above Earth. The amount of torque you can generate is related to the amount of force you apply times the length of the lever; applying force at the end of a long lever gives you more torque than applying the same amount of force on a short lever. So my father jammed the end of this long screwdriver under the lip of the filter. Uncle Frank then wrapped a rag around the handle and started yanking down on it as hard as he could, grunting and cursing under his breath with each tug: *"Ungh! Ungh! Ungh!"* He did that for nearly a minute, and finally the filter broke torque and popped out.

As I looked at that handrail attached to this $100 million instrument inside this $1 billion telescope, after fourteen years of highly specialized training from the most advanced minds in the history of space exploration, all I could picture was my uncle Frank, under the hood of his car, covered in grease, cursing and grunting and yanking on the end of that giant screwdriver. I thought, *This one's for you, Uncle Frank*. I grabbed the top of it and I rocked it back a couple times and I yanked it hard and *bam!* it came off. Clean. No debris. No punctured space suit.

"Awesome job," Burbank said. "We're back in with the regularly scheduled programming."

Bueno took the handrail and put it in a disposal bag. I didn't care what else happened, I was fixing that telescope. Nothing in the world—nothing in the universe—could stop me.

I drove the guide stud anchors. One, two, three, four, they all went in flush. Perfect. I put the capture plate on. It fit, and I cinched it down. Perfect. I took the foil cutter and I sheared off the label exposing the screws underneath. Perfect.

Now I'd reached the big moment: 111 tiny screws and washers to remove without making a single mistake. I grabbed my mini power tool, I pulled the trigger, and . . . nothing happened. I pulled it again. Still nothing. It was dead. I said, "Aw, for Pete's sake." Bueno and I looked at each other. *What else could go wrong?* Fortunately, this wasn't a big deal. Either the battery had died or we'd charged the wrong one the night before, but the spare was in the air lock and I needed to get more oxygen anyway, so it was one more trip across the payload bay for me.

As I was making my way back, two things happened. First, the sun came out. The cold and the darkness had passed and everything was warm and bright and clear again. Second, as I was moving along that edge and looking over the side of the shuttle, I realized that I wasn't scared. I'd been back and forth so many times that this treacherous path wasn't so treacherous anymore. I realized that my doubts and fears had been totally wrong. I was a spacewalker. I *was* the right guy for the job. They *had* picked the right person for this. Because being the right person isn't about being perfect; it's about being able to handle whatever life throws at you. I'd faced every astronaut's worst nightmare, and with the help of my team, I pulled myself out of it. And if that problem with the handrail had never happened, I never would have known I had that in me.

I zipped down the side of the shuttle, put a new battery in the mini power tool, pumped up my oxygen tank, and went back out like a superhero to fix that telescope. And we did it. We hit a couple of bumps, but the rest of the day just went. The screws came out, the panel came off, the old power supply came out, the new power supply went in, and we closed it up.

Once we were done, the team at Goddard performed an aliveness test to see if the STIS was operating again. It was. Everybody started cheering and high-fiving each other, saying "Great job" and "Way to go." I felt a huge

weight lifted off my shoulders. Then, while the big celebration was going on, I glanced down at my glove and
noticed something: There was a tiny rip in my space
suit glove. It was only in the outer fabric. It hadn't gone
through the other layers yet, but if we'd seen that rip earlier, that would have been it. Ceccacci would have aborted
the spacewalk and brought us in immediately. The whole
space walk would have been over before it started.

After we closed the telescope doors, Bueno was at the
back of the payload bay finishing up, and I went back
into the air lock to do an inventory and stow things away.
Scooter came over the comm.

"Mass, what are you doing?"

"I'm getting the air lock ready."

"Is there anything you're doing now that can't wait?"

"No."

"Well, why don't you go outside and enjoy the view?"

This was the commander ordering me, so I figured I'd
better do as I was told.

"Okay."

I went back out, up to the top of the payload bay,
clipped my safety tether to a handrail, and I just . . . let
go. I stretched out and relaxed, the same way you'd float
on your back in the ocean on a warm summer day, and
looked at the Earth below. The view I'd dreamed of when
watching *The Right Stuff* more than twenty-five years earlier could not come close to this. We were coming over

Hawaii, a few tiny islands alone in this brilliant expanse of blue. It was beautiful again. Magnificent. I wasn't stealing a glance at the planet while I was supposed to be working, and I wasn't inside, craning my neck to look through a window. I could turn my head in every direction and drink it all in.

We hit Southern California and San Diego; then Las Vegas and Phoenix started whipping by. When I was twenty-one years old, I watched *The Right Stuff* from the balcony of the Floral Park theater on Long Island and saw a sliver of the Earth through the tiny window in John Glenn's capsule. I decided I wouldn't be happy until I saw it for myself, and here I was, except that the view was a thousand times more spectacular than anything he witnessed on that flight. Life doesn't give you many perfect moments. This was one of them. This was my reward, my gift, a few precious minutes to lie back and look at the most perfect, most beautiful thing in the universe. Then, as we came up on the East Coast, I felt that chill in my bones telling me that night was on its way. Out of the corner of my eye I saw a dark line creeping toward me westward across the Atlantic, and I knew it was time to go back in.

It was time to come home.

22

GROUNDED

Coming back to Earth is hard. It's an adjustment. After Bueno and I finished the STIS repair, John and Drew had a successful final space walk. The next day, we said goodbye to the Hubble, sending it off on its way to unlock the secrets of the universe. We had our normal day off and went through our final inspections. Whenever I could, I'd steal a few minutes to go up to the flight deck and look out the window. Outside the window, I could see the Ku-band antenna, covered in gold foil, moving and reconfiguring itself. That's how it works: It locks onto the signal from a communications satellite and tracks it to keep us connected to the ground. Anytime it loses the signal, it pivots and swivels around until it finds the signal again.

Watching the antenna swivel around, with the Earth passing below, I had a feeling I don't think I'd ever had before: satisfaction. I could relax. I was finished. For

five years, the Hubble had consumed my every waking
moment, and now all that stress and responsibility had
floated away. It was a huge relief not to have to think
about it anymore. It was done, and I could feel good about
it. And I wasn't satisfied only with the mission. My whole
life I'd been restless. I always had to do more, reach for the
next challenge, the next opportunity. Now I could stop
and take a breath. I'd done everything I'd set out to do.

The morning we were supposed to fly home, there was
bad weather over Florida and we got waved off a day.

The next morning, Florida was still clouded over, but
we couldn't stay any longer. We were diverted to land at
Edwards Air Force Base in California. Our families would
meet us in Houston. This time I was on the flight deck for
the trip home, so I got to see everything: the Earth getting bigger and bigger as we flew lower and lower, the
shuttle's nose and tail glowing red-orange hot. There had
been an ever-present worry about entry ever since *Columbia,* but as soon as we came out of the darkness over
the Pacific and I could see the California coast lit up in the
daylight, I knew Scooter was going to get us home safely.

Two days later I was in my driveway, feeling out of
sorts. During your first week back, your hand-eye coor-
dination is completely messed up. Your sense of balance is
thrown. Your spine is still settling back together, and that
can be uncomfortable. You're not supposed to drive or
work heavy equipment for three days. Part of it is great, of

course: seeing your family, having this wonderful feeling of accomplishment. But then you drive up to the house, and real life is there waiting for you: Some shingles over the garage need to be fixed, the pool needs to be cleaned. People always ask me if I miss being in space. "Only when I'm mowing the lawn," I say.

Fortunately for me, even though the flight had ended, the mission was far from over. When we landed at Edwards, one of the administrator's assistants was waiting for us with a copy of the *Washington Post*. There was a big photo, above the fold, of me in my space suit with a big smile in front of the telescope in the payload bay; Megan or John or Scooter had taken it during my last space walk. Hubble was a big story. People wanted to hear about it, learn about it. Because of my experiences and thanks to Twitter, I wound up handling many of the media appearances.

From the beginning, my love of space was shaped by the way astronauts are portrayed in the media and in pop culture. Watching the moon landing with Walter Cronkite, poring through old *Life* magazines, going to the movies to see *The Right Stuff* and *Apollo 13*—those things changed how I felt when I looked up at the sky and dreamed of going there, and I remember that every time I'm given the opportunity to step in front of an audience.

On July 8, 2011, at 11:29 A.M., Gabby and I were standing outside the Saturn V building at Kennedy Space Center, in an area called the Banana Creek viewing site, for the final flight of the thirty-year shuttle program. The space shuttle *Atlantis* was on launchpad 39A, ready to take the crew of STS-135 up to deliver a year's worth of clothing, food, and equipment to the astronauts on the space station. It was completely surreal that it was happening. When I arrived at NASA in 1996, I figured I'd fly four or five times at least. The shuttle program was thriving. The space shuttle was space travel. There was no reason to think it would ever come to an end. But it had, and what did that mean? Were we supposed to be celebrating the shuttle's achievements? Sad that it hadn't lived up to its promise? I didn't know what to feel about it. I don't think anyone did.

The launch of the final shuttle mission came with the usual editorials and news segments about why we go to space and whether the expense of the shuttle was worth the return. When *USA Today* published a look back at the shuttle program's triumphs and tragedies, a friend of mine brought me a copy. The tragedies it listed, of course, were the *Challenger* and *Columbia* accidents and the fourteen lives that were lost. As the triumph of the shuttle program, the article cited this:

> On May 17, 2009, floating 353 miles above the surface of the Earth, astronaut Michael Massimino put his gloved hand around a balky handrail obstructing repairs and ripped it off the $1.5 billion Hubble Space Telescope. Only an astronaut could have done this.

Flattered as I was, the point the article was trying to make wasn't really about me. It was about the importance of astronauts. It was the same conclusion we came to after researching the robot mission to Hubble. Unmanned space travel is a great first step; lunar probes and Mars Rovers are excellent tools for scouting a path to explore—but you still need people to do the exploring. What was accomplished on those Hubble servicing missions—upgrading the instruments, repairing the STIS, yanking off that handrail—would have been impossible without astronauts, and we couldn't have done it without the shuttle.

There's an ongoing debate about the most important legacy of the shuttle, whether it's deploying and servicing the Hubble Space Telescope or building and supplying the International Space Station. Whenever I'm asked, I say the greatest thing the shuttle did was to put a lot of people in space—fifty, sometimes sixty people a year when the program was at its peak. Every person who goes to space, every person who gets to peek around the next corner, is someone with the potential to help change our perspective, change our relationship to the planet, change our understanding of our place in the universe. Which is why we go to space to begin with.

I knew I was never going back, but a few weeks after STS-135 launched, it was made official. I was pulled off active flight status. I was still an astronaut, but I wasn't returning to space again—and no more hours in the T-38, either. I was grounded. After his one flight on 125, Ray J had left the astronaut office for Ellington, where he became head of flight operations. He called me up one day and told me he'd seen that I was being taken off the flight list at the end of September. "What do you want to do?" he asked.

"I want to fly."

So, for my last couple of weeks, Ray J took me flying. We went out and did acrobatics in the practice area over the Gulf of Mexico. We went cloud surfing, did loops and barrel rolls and touch-and-goes on the runway at Ellington. I flew as fast and as high as I'll ever fly again.

My first year as an astronaut, Carola and I had family in for Christmas. I was on the last T-38 flight before the holiday, and I told them, "Hey, I'm flying today. Why don't you come by and I'll show you some airplanes." A bunch of folks came out, and I showed them around. Daniel was seventeen months old at the time. I was a brand-new astronaut with this baby boy with curly golden hair. I remember he was wearing this jumpsuit with dinosaurs on it. He was getting the hang of walking and had just started forming real words and he was all over the place, baby talking, "Ba ba ba ba ba," like he was the one giving the tour of the airplanes.

When it was time for everyone to go, I still had to change. Daniel wanted to stay with me, so I said, "I'll take him home." I brought him back to the locker room and he toddled around, getting into everything while I changed. Once I was ready, I called him over and bent down and gave him my little finger. He took it and we walked out together, past all the planes in the hangar, saying "Bye bye" and "Merry Christmas" to everyone. Then we got in my car and drove home.

For my last flight, Daniel was grown. He was sixteen, almost a man. Gabby was away at college. Daniel and Carola and my mom and my sister came out to Ellington for the occasion. It was September 30, 2011, a Friday, the last flight of the day. Ray J took me out for some acrobatics and a quick trip over to Lake Charles. Everyone was going to go out to dinner afterward, but I still had to change and clear out my locker. "Whatever you leave here we're going to throw out," they told me. I said to Daniel, "Why don't you stay and help me clean out my locker? Then I'll drive us to dinner."

Daniel sat with me while I packed up some maps and old boots and a couple of flight suits. There was some chitchat here and there, but it was mostly me and him at the end of it, just like we were at the beginning. I closed the locker, spun the combination, and locked it. Right in front of me on the locker was my name tag, MIKE MASSIMINO, JSC, HOUSTON. During my time there'd been so many names on those lockers. John Young. John Glenn. Rick Husband and Ilan Ramon. At one point or another all those names had come off, and now it was time for mine to come off, too. I looked at my name tag and thought, *This is the coolest thing I'll ever do. I got to fly with my heroes, and now it's done.* Then I ripped it off, leaving an empty locker with a strip of Velcro on the front for them to give to the next guy. Then Daniel and I headed out, making the same walk we'd made fifteen years before. Only, it wasn't Christmas this time. It was late at night, the sun going down and everybody gone for the day. We walked out through the empty hangar, past the rows of quiet planes, climbed into our car, and went home.

AROUND THE NEXT CORNER

Being grounded was a hard transition for me. I'd been dreaming of going to space since I was a kid. I'd never really thought about what I was going to do afterward. Once you leave active flight status, you're supposed to transition to a managerial role or say your goodbyes. I didn't want to be management, but I wasn't ready to leave, either. I hung around the office for a while, making public relations videos, doing guest spots on TV, helping to train new astronauts, handling whatever I was assigned to handle. I was in denial for a long time. I knew that things were winding down, but I wasn't taking any decisive steps to do something else. Part of me felt like nothing I did could possibly top what I'd already done. But part of me knew that wasn't true. I did want to do other things, tackle other challenges, but it was hard to admit that to myself.

There came a point, looking around the office, when I knew it was time. Kevin Kregel had retired; he was flying commercial for Southwest Airlines. Scorch had left to fly for FedEx. Digger had been gone since 2004; he moved to Colorado and became a motivational speaker. Scooter had left in 2010 to work for an aerospace technology company. Steve Smith and Rick Linnehan and Nancy Currie were here and there, serving in different managerial jobs. John Grunsfeld was leaving for an administrative role at NASA headquarters in DC; I'm pretty sure he'll end up running the whole place someday. Bueno and Drew flew again on station assembly flights and were both still active. Megan was still active, too, but taking time off to have a baby. I was coming up on my fiftieth birthday. Younger people were coming in and stepping up. I needed to make a decision. I thought a lot about the talk Neil Armstrong gave to us my first week at NASA: The important thing in life is having a passion, something you really love doing, and you take joy in the fact that you get to wake up every day and do it.

I began to realize academia made the most sense for me. I'd enjoyed teaching during my time at Rice and at Georgia Tech. In December 2011, Rice University reached out to NASA, looking for someone to be the executive director of the Rice Space Institute. They wanted someone to beef up their program and coordinate its research and activities more closely with the work being done at the Johnson Space Center. I applied for the job, got it, and the astronaut office agreed to loan me out; my salary and benefits would still be paid by NASA, but I would work at the university. I led a few seminars, helped to develop the curriculum. It was a great way to ease back into university life. Not long after, my alma mater Columbia started asking if I wanted to come back to the engineering school as a visiting professor, still on loan from NASA. As it happened, Daniel was starting at Columbia as a freshman in the fall of 2013. Gabby was starting her junior year at Sarah Lawrence up in Bronxville, just outside New York City. With the kids gone and the shuttle program over, Carola and I didn't have much keeping us in Houston. After fifteen months at Rice, I took the visiting professorship offer and we moved back to New York.

In the fall of 2014, I left NASA to become a full-time professor at Columbia. My main class, and my most popular one, is Introduction to Human Space Flight. The way I see it, I'm training my replacements. My job is to inspire them, to show them what it takes to live and work and accomplish great things under brutally difficult circumstances. I take them from the story of Ernest Shackleton to life on the International Space Station and cover everything in between. Not all of my students will become astronauts—most of them won't—but they may help the environment or cure a disease or create some lifesaving technology. The same lessons still apply. I try to teach them to be socially useful, to put their talents in the service of the public good. And I'm not only talking to the students in my class. I travel to high schools across the country, talking to young people by the thousands, encouraging them to go to college, to challenge themselves, to follow their dreams. To get past whatever hurdles are in their way. To get back up when they fall down. To keep going and going, working harder and harder and running faster and faster until one day, before they know it, they'll find themselves flying through the air. The hand of a giant science-fiction monster will reach down and grab them by the chest and hurl them up and up and up, out to the furthest limits of the human imagination, where they'll take the next giant leap of the greatest adventure mankind has ever known.

Still to this day I look back over the obstacles and hurdles I've overcome, and I see that six-year-old boy standing there with his Astronaut Snoopy in his little spaceman outfit that his mom made for him, and I'm so glad he never gave up.

ACKNOWLEDGMENTS

Writing a book for young adults was a new experience for me, one that would have never been possible without the help of many of my colleagues, family members, and friends. Thanks to the entire Random House Children's Books team, especially my editor at Delacorte Press, Beverly Horowitz, who had the vision to see that *Spaceman* could appeal to and inspire many young people, and then had the patience to help me write this book. Thanks to my literary agent, Peter McGuigan, and his team at Foundry Literary & Media, who reached out on my behalf to make my wish of writing a young adult book a reality. Many thanks also go to those who helped me craft the stories in the adult version of *Spaceman* by cowriting, editing, and reviewing: Tanner Colby, Kevin Doughten, Jessica Marinaccio, Megan McArthur Behnken, and Frances Massimino. Many of those stories and themes are present in this version of the book. Most of all, my thanks go to those readers who reached out to me to tell me how much they enjoyed the adult version of *Spaceman* and how a young adult version could help inspire many young people to pursue their dreams. Their kind words motivated me, and I am very grateful that they took the time to write them.

ABOUT THE AUTHOR

MIKE MASSIMINO served as a NASA astronaut from
1996 to 2014. On his two space flights to the Hubble Space
Telescope, Mike and his crews set team records for spacewalking time, and he became the first person to tweet
from space. He has played himself on the CBS sitcom *The
Big Bang Theory,* was featured in the IMAX film *Hubble
3D,* and has appeared frequently in television documen-
taries and on late-night talk shows and news programs. A
graduate of Columbia University and MIT, Mike lives in
New York City, where he is a professor at Columbia and an
advisor at the Intrepid Sea, Air & Space Museum and an
in-demand public speaker.

MikeMassimino.com